C000173085

"A sparkling and thorough ....
that tell us to be true to ourselves. Each chapter p...
gospel insights into our deepest longings for authenticity and acceptance. This warm and often humorous book blends a liberating biblical anthropology with culturally rich insights into our quest for identity. It deserves to be widely circulated."

RICHARD CUNNINGHAM, Director, UCCF: the Christian Unions

"For many today, the often-unspoken purpose of life is to discover who you are and express that to the world. Matt Fuller explains the meaning of the popular slogan "Be true to yourself" within the larger framework of God's word and its view of our world. This book is helpful, relevant and full of thought-provoking cultural analysis."

TREVIN WAX, Author, *This Is Our Time* and *Gospel Centered Teaching*

"Every teenager and twentysomething is looking for their identity. Our selfie-obsessed culture tells us that to find it, we need to look within, follow our hearts and be true to ourselves. But Matt Fuller offers a better way... because he offers Jesus' way: deny yourself and follow Christ. This is a book for the times and a book my generation desperately needs as they navigate our culture. I'm so grateful for *Be True to Yourself*!"

JAQUELLE CROWE FERRIS, Author, *This Changes Eveything*; Founder and COO, The Young Writer

"This pithy and culturally incisive book is a must-read for Christians of all ages. Matt Fuller's theological, biblical and pastoral insights offer a life-giving alternative to a culture that is over-promising and under-delivering."

STEPHEN McALPINE, City Bible Forum

"I'm grateful for Matt Fuller's timely new book. *Be True to Yourself* is a strong antidote to a mindset—once a cultural vice, now a heroic virtue—that fires our imaginations and ruins our lives. On page after page, Matt unveils a counterintuitive secret: following your heart will enslave you, but following Jesus will free you."

MATT SMETHURST, Managing Editor, The Gospel Coalition; Author, *Before You Open Your Bible*

"An extraordinarily important book! Matt so helpfully tackles many of the lies of our current society and shines the truth of God's word in a compelling, concise and captivating way. A must-read for people in our church today."

PAUL DALE, Senior Pastor, Church by the Bridge, Kirribilli, Sydney

"Matt Fuller's use of story makes him an engaging writer, and his pastoral experience and compassion are evident on every page. *Be True to Yourself* will help the reader to better understand the different voices being fed to us in our culture, and to gain a deeper love and trust for God's freeing voice instead."

JANE TOOHER, Lecturer, Moore College

"Absolutely brilliant! I loved reading *Be True to Yourself*: it's biblically rich, emotionally intelligent, culturally perceptive and beautifully written. Matt addresses many of the most powerful current challenges to biblical Christianity, including those around sexuality and gender, with deep compassion and impressive clarity."

RICHARD COEKIN, Senior Pastor, Dundonald Church; Executive Director, Co-Mission Network, London

"This brief book by Matt Fuller is a helpful guide through the maze of messages we all receive in our modern age. It's deep yet approachable, and kept me turning the pages for the solutions offered in the gospel. I recommend this for anyone looking to understand themselves more truthfully."

ADAM MABRY, Lead Pastor, Aletheia Church, Boston; Author, *The Art of Rest*

"Matt Fuller angles the reader's gaze away from introspection and toward our loving heavenly Father. This is a timely, smart, practical and important book that helps followers of Jesus focus primarily on Christ's supremacy and the weight of the gospel."

SHELBY ABBOTT, Campus Minister, Cru; Author, *Pressure Points: A Guide to Navigating Student Stress*

"Matt Fuller has the ability to tap into our culture and our hearts, and then let the word of God and the grace of God expose, reorient, guide and comfort us with tremendously helpful insights. But you know a book is good when you want to side with Jesus because you're persuaded again that his way is the best way."

RAY GALEA, Lead Pastor, Multicultural Bible Ministry

"Matt Fuller is a deft theologian who has his finger on the pulse of the culture. His cultural intelligence, his deep knowledge of the Scriptures, his logical train of argument and his winsome prose have together produced a gracious and engaging answer to the fleeting orthodoxies of the day. *Be True to Yourself* will prove to be a go-to help for all who strive to communicate the gospel—and a lifeline to those adrift amid the evanescent logics of the twenty-first century."

R. KENT HUGHES, Senior Pastor Emeritus of College Church, Wheaton, Illinois

"Matt Fuller's book is a wonderful reminder of what matters most—the glory of God (not the glory of me)—and an invitation to look at Jesus, where we find our greatest joy. With clarity and depth of insight, Matt points us to the bigger truths of Scripture that need to capture our hearts. I loved it!"

JENNY SALT, Dean of Students, Sydney Missionary and Bible College, Sydney, Australia

"This book offers a beautiful and hope-filled biblical response to the unbearable pressures our culture has placed upon us. Packed full of insight and loaded with illustrations and commentary on our culture, it helps us understand both where we have been led astray and then how the gospel fully answers our quest for significance and meaning. A must-read for all in the church if we want to understand ourselves and our world better."

NEIL POWELL, Pastor, City Church Birmingham

"Matt manages to speak honestly about everyday life, to engage genuinely with modern culture and to inspire powerfully with God's view of who we really are. Read this book and grow into the person you were always meant to be."

JASON ROACH, Senior Minister, The Bridge: Battersea Community Church, London

"This is such a liberating book. It doesn't settle for a small definition of who we are. This pushes us to a deeper understanding of who we truly are made to be. I hope it helps many to find the freedom God has in store for us."

JONTY ALLCOCK, Pastor, The Globe Church, London

MATT FULLER

BE
TRUE
TO
YOUR
SELF

thegoodbook
COMPANY

For Nathan, Lucy, Rufus, Eliza, Sam and Ollie.
I hope this helps in a confusing time.

Be True to Yourself
© Matt Fuller, 2020

Published by:
The Good Book Company

thegoodbook.com | www.thegoodbook.co.uk
thegoodbook.com.au | thegoodbook.co.nz | thegoodbook.co.in

ISBN: 9781784982911 | Printed in the UK

Design by André Parker

CONTENTS

Introduction   9

1. To Thine Own Self Be True   11

2. Finding Ourselves in Reflecting God   27

3. Finding Ourselves in Knowing Others   43

4. Finding Ourselves in Seeing Christ   57

5. Identity: Certainty > Self-creation   73

6. Gender and Sexuality: How Should I
   Define Myself?   85

7. Sex: The Hunger of Self-gratification?   101

8. Relationships: Deny Yourself to Find
   Yourself   119

9. Community: There Can Be No
   Losers in Church   135

10. Online: True to Selfie in a
    Virtual World   153

11. I'm Not the Messiah…
    (but I Want to Become Like Him)   171

INTRODUCTION

INTRODUCTION

I am amazing. If you've never met me, don't just take my word for it—others think so too. I went into my favourite local coffee shop the other day, and there was a sign up in the toilet:

WHO IS AWESOME?
YOU
ARE AWESOME

(It was definitely more appealing than the previous sign that had been there, which rather aggressively demanded, "Now wash your hands".)

It was only a sign in a bathroom. Yet it's also a belief that most of us live by. It's a belief that I often live by. But it's not without its complications. And that's why I wrote this book.

Being told that we're wonderful is certainly not a *new* idea—L'Oréal has been selling cosmetics "because you're worth it" for almost 50 years. But it's definitely a very *current* idea. And it's become our motto not just for whether we buy a certain shampoo but for how we do life. If I'm awesome, then I need to make sure I find myself, be myself, express myself—no matter what other people may think.

In other words, you need to "be true to yourself". That's the way to be happy. It's an idea that is posted on social media, expressed in ads, celebrated in songs, taught in schools and quietly believed in churches.

And it's right. Sort of. Being true to yourself really is the most satisfying way to live. It really can make you happy. It's a philosophy you really can live by. But only if you know who you really are. It means listening to the voice of your Creator and living out his design for your life.

Otherwise, we may simply be self-deceived. I was struck by how contemporary these words sounded despite being written 140 years ago by the Russian novelist Fyodor Dostoevsky in *The Brothers Karamazov*:

"Above all, don't lie to yourself. The man who lies to himself and listens to his own lie comes to such a pass that he cannot distinguish the truth within him, or around him, and so loses all respect for himself and for others. And having no respect, he ceases to love."

Could it be that in our culture, where we turn within to find truth, we no longer know what is really, objectively true at all?

Yes, be true to yourself—but that means be true to who God says you are. Listen to the voice of your Creator and live out his design for your life. That's the route to real happiness.

1. TO THINE OWN SELF BE TRUE

"This above all: to thine own self be true."
William Shakespeare, *Hamlet*

Just a few days before the start of the 1998 Tour de France, a large haul of performance-enhancing drugs was found in the support car for Team Festina. It was a discovery that led to the exposure of a widescale doping programme within the team.

As the scandal unfolded, it emerged that *every* member of Team Festina had been using drugs. Except, that is, for one: Christophe Bassons.

Despite coming under pressure from the management and his teammates, he did not cheat. Although he received no share of their winning bonuses, he did not cheat. He was publicly humiliated by Lance Armstrong, the dominant rider at the time, but he did not cheat. He was threatened with being dropped from the team, but he did not cheat (and so he was indeed dropped).

Later, it became apparent that Bassons was in the right, and the rest of the team and many other cyclists had been guilty of taking illegal steroids. When asked how he had resisted the enormous pressure to join in with the cheating, he observed, "I don't think I was courageous not to take drugs. I'd had a balanced upbringing, lots of love in my life, no void which made me want to dope" (Matthew Syed, *The Greatest*, p 130).

In other words: *I wanted to be true to myself.*

If you're anything like me, when you read a story like that, you want to give Bassons a little cheer. "Good for you!" we think. "If only everyone behaved like that, then the world would be a better place."

As we come to think about what it means to "be true to yourself", it's clear that the phrase can mean some very positive things.

But it can also mean, well... a lot of different things.

Let me give you five overlapping ways that I think people use that phrase. Why not put a mental (or real) tick next to the ones you agree with?

1. Integrity

This is what we've seen with Bassons: he was "true to himself" in the sense that he resisted doping and the associated pressure to fit in, stuck to his principles, and acted with integrity. That's what playwright William

Shakespeare meant 450 years ago when he had a character in *Hamlet* advise:

"This above all: to thine own self be true,
 And it must follow, as the night the day,
 Thou canst not then be false to any man."

In this sense, being honest is obviously a good and noble thing. We might wish of a politician, "Don't pander to the powerful just to advance your career; do the right thing". We celebrate when people are true to their conscience and act with integrity.

2. Express the Real You

This is the idea that to be true to yourself you need to strip away all the layers of conformity that you have had imposed upon you by society over the years, and find the real you deep inside. You have to look inside to discover who you truly are.

What is most valuable to you? What values do you cherish? Which people do you identify with? When you have worked out who you are, then live that way—no matter what others say. Haters gonna hate. Just ignore them.

In our culture, conformity is seen as a negative thing, but trusting our own internal instincts and ideas is seen as a positive thing. So I read a fairly typical magazine article by one twenty-something journalist who said of her peers, "We don't feel the need to stay in one relationship, *just because society dictates it*" (Hannah Rogers, *The Sunday*

Times Magazine 05 Aug 17, p 14, my italics). We are told, "Ignore the voices outside and follow the real you inside". (Although of course, there's a certain irony in the way that "Be true to yourself" is itself a worldview imposed on us by loud voices in our culture!)

3. I Feel; Therefore I Am

Not only is who we are inside something to be expressed, but our feelings inside are something to be followed. In 21st-century Western culture, we increasingly make decisions based on what feels right. In this sense, being true to ourselves is a maxim by which to navigate life— and the way we know who we are is by what we feel.

Does something make me feel happy, or free, or radical? Then I assume it's good. If, on the other hand, something feels like hard work, or makes me feel constrained or feels traditional... then I assume it's bad. A couple of decades ago, I could come out with a statement, and someone who disagreed with me might say, "Is that true?" Now they're more likely to say, "That doesn't resonate with me".

This way of making decisions has become prominent in politics too. During an interview in the lead-up to the Brexit referendum, the UK's then Justice Secretary, Michael Gove, didn't trouble to engage with the economic predictions of what would happen if the nation voted to leave. Instead, he dismissed the argument with "People in this country have had enough of experts".

In the US, too, emotional statements are increasingly taking the place of reasoned ones. One comment that captures this attitude was made by a member of Congress on prime-time TV:

"I think that there's a lot of people more concerned about being precisely, factually and semantically correct than about being morally right."

Regardless of your political views, it's a striking way of making decisions: you can ignore facts if they don't accord with your personal values or morals.

For some people, being true to yourself means listening to your feelings regardless of facts. If what you feel inside conflicts with facts in the outside world, then you need to change the world!

4. Live for Yourself, Not for Others

In this sense, being true to yourself means refusing to be moulded and squashed by other peoples' expectations. Former First Lady Michelle Obama tells women:

"Our first job in life as women ... is to get to know ourselves. And I think a lot of times we don't do that. We spend a lot of time pleasing, satisfying, looking out into the world to define who we are—listening to the messages, the images, the limited definitions that people have of who we are." [1]

Her good friend Oprah Winfrey agrees:

"The fullness of our humanity can be expressed only when we are true to ourselves ... Anything less is a faked life. To be authentic is the highest form of praise. You're fulfilling your mission and purpose on earth when you honour the real you." [2]

Living with a constant desire to please other people is often unhealthy and usually exhausting. Many of us can think of parents who have tried to force their children down a route or career path that the kids didn't want (we may be that kid or those parents). There comes a time when they might need to say, "Mum and Dad, thanks for your counsel, but I'm not like you, and I don't want to be a doctor; I want to be a musician".

Even more common is the influence that peer pressure exerts upon all of us—whether it's the teenager under pressure to take drugs to fit in, the twenty-something under pressure to take an expensive holiday they can't afford, or the middle-aged couple desperate to get their child into a particular school.

Every single one of us has known a time when we compromised a little just to conform. Isn't it more heroic and more liberating to say, "I did it my way"?

5. Overcome Injustice and Be Kind

In our society there's an increasing awareness that some groups and minorities have been treated appallingly in the past—and we are determined that this should not happen again.

So we celebrate heroes such as Nelson Mandela, who refused to accept apartheid in South Africa and so suffered 27 years of imprisonment for fighting for his beliefs. In a case like that, it really was morally imperative that he remain true to his own beliefs and not conform.

At a day-to-day level, we now celebrate cultural diversity in food, music and clothing rather than preferring people to conform to established practices and fashions. A belief in self-expression is often allied with a movement towards greater inclusivity in society. Minorities are increasingly protected and celebrated, rather than marginalised and discriminated against. This is all good!

Much of our popular culture reinforces this theme. I have a personal weakness for the film *The Greatest Showman*. I'm a sucker for its upbeat message, good music and extraordinary dance sequences. It also has an enormously contemporary message in the way it celebrates the courage and mutual acceptance of circus owner P.T. Barnum's troupe of "freaks". We find it uplifting that, as the storyline develops, these "misfits" overcome those who harass them for being different. We are naturally on their side, and so we cheer when they sing in the face of hostility, "I am who I'm meant to be. This is me." We hope that the wealthy white writer and poor black trapeze artist can cross boundaries, "rewrite the stars" and be together. If being "true to yourself" = overcoming fearful prejudice, then that is likely to be a good thing.

So, how many did you get? Four or five ticks? Whatever you think of those definitions, at the very least I hope that it's shown you that the phrase "Be true to yourself" doesn't really mean one fixed thing. It means lots of different things to lots of different people. Many of these ideas are ones which Christians can happily affirm.

And yet...

As a phrase, being "true to self" does raise all sorts of questions.

Who Is the "Who" to Whom I Must Be True?

All of us have conflicting feelings, so how do we know which ones to prioritise?

On January 1st it may be my overwhelming desire to get healthy. So I join a gym, buy a vegan cookbook and throw away boxes of chocolates I received for Christmas. Yet on January 2nd I can't be bothered to go out, and all I want is to order takeaway pizza. Which desire is my "true" one? It's very hard to build an identity on feelings that can change on a whim.

We can stretch that out over decades as well. Should I be true to how I felt or will feel as an eight-year-old, an eighteen-year-old, or an eighty-year-old? You see, what I think keeps changing. I look back on some of the things that I thought (and wore) as an eighteen-year-old with horror. I imagine that in ten years' time I'll howl with laughter at some of the things I wear and think today.

How seriously should I take my opinion when I expect it to change?

We see something of this tension in the UK Girl Guides' updated membership pledge. Since 2013, when someone joins the organisation aged seven, rather than promising to "love my God" and "serve my country", they pledge to "be true to myself and develop my beliefs". But how do you decide which of your beliefs to stay true to, and which of your beliefs need to develop? (I think that when I was seven years old, being true to myself would have meant stuffing my face with as many sweets as possible, never doing schoolwork and watching TV all day long. I'm glad that my parents prevented me from living as I desired!)

On one level, it's a good thing to be open to changing your beliefs. But it's very hard to build your life and identity upon something which is constantly in flux. If I keep on changing, to which self must I be true? The question *Who am I?* never has a definitive answer in the modern world.

A further problem is that sometimes we don't know ourselves very well.

In the West there exists the well-documented "Better than average" syndrome:

- 98% of the UK population think that they have an above-average IQ.

- 95% of the population think that they have above-average looks.

- 98% think that they're in the top 50% of the nicest people in the UK.

No matter what trait you ask people about, the results are largely the same. Researchers call this "illusory superiority"—the need to feel good by looking down on others.

At the risk of pricking the bubble, I must tell you that the stats suggest that half us are less intelligent, uglier and nastier than we realise. Ouch! (Although most of us reading this will think that half doesn't include us.)

But it raises this question: how can we be true to ourselves when half of us can't even be honest with ourselves?

Can I Really Survive Without the Opinions of Others?

Oprah says that the only opinion that matters is hers; she doesn't need other people to affirm her choices or her work. However, all of us know that there's a sense in which we cannot survive without validation and approval from outside of ourselves.

If a composer is told by everyone that their music is awful, it's hard to keep going. If every painting an artist produces is laughed at as pathetic, they will eventually give up. If I write a book and sell zero copies, I won't be motivated to have another go.

Or what if you work in an office and your boss tells you that every piece of work you do is terrible? Are you really going to say, "Well, I don't care about your opinion. Mine is the only one that matters"?

If we're honest, we'll recognise that it's impossible to live without taking into account the opinion of others!

Any attempt to do so will eventually leave us miserable. We exist in a web of relationships—we're simply not wired to rely upon our own verdict.

Will Being True to Myself Make Me Happy?

Sociologists are now raising the alarm over the rise of mental-health problems in those born in the last 25 years—a generation raised on the mantra of "be true to yourself".

In her book *iGen*, psychologist Jean Twenge analyses vast amounts of data and concludes that this generation is suffering the worst mental-health crisis in decades.

- One in eight people under the age of 19 have a mental-health disorder.

- One in four of 17-19-year-old girls suffer with a mental disorder, of whom half said they had self-harmed or attempted suicide.

- The UK government is now introducing compulsory lessons for four-year-old children on how to handle depression.

Now, there are complicated reasons for this phenomenon,

but Twenge argues that a greater focus on the self is one key cause.

So, in simple terms, will being true to myself actually make me happy? Perhaps counterintuitively, the answer according to the emerging data is no.

Do I Really Want *Everyone* to Be True to Themselves?

Most of us are happy to encourage others to be true to themselves… as long as the self to whom they are being true is rational, kind and decent. We want people to be true to themselves as long as they are people with similar values to us. But what if they're not?

What about the brutal dictator, willing to any undertake any corruption, commit any crime or kill any opponents in order to stay in power? Or, more domestically, what about the person who barges to the front of the queue and says, "I can't bear waiting in line"?

Maybe the soundbite just needs some nuance: "Be true to yourself, as long as no one else is harmed".

But even that doesn't quite work. If a friend bails on us because they "can't really be bothered tonight", we can't really claim they're causing us harm. But their decision is still upsetting.

Think back to the example of Christophe Bassons. The reason that people admire him is not primarily that he was true to himself. Rather, it was that, unlike the other riders, he did the right thing by keeping the rules. Lance Armstrong was also being "true to himself" by doping—he was simply following his greatest desire for victory and fame.

In reality, we don't admire Bassons for being true to himself but for being true to an objective standard. He was true to a higher truth. He kept the rules.

If we take a moment to dig a little deeper, what we're actually saying is that for most people "Be true to yourself" means *express your own beliefs and practices as long as they conform to a higher cultural truth.* Or, to put it simply: "We want you to be true to yourself, as long as your truth is acceptable to us."

With views and practices that we like, we say, "Be true to yourself and don't worry what anyone else thinks".

With views and practices that we think are wrong, we say, "Your views are horrible and you need to change".

So we like the fact that Christophe Bassons trusts his instincts, but we don't like it when Lance Armstrong does. The great cry of our age comes with a significant caveat: "You must be true to yourself" (as long as I don't dislike your views and behaviour).

"You must be true to yourself" (as long as you are pro-immigration...).

"You must be true to yourself" (as long as you are pro/anti globalisation...).

"You must be true to yourself" (as long as you're not from a privileged background...).

Without the "higher truth", we simply don't know what to do when there is a clash of views. It can get very confusing. Take this tricky example: recently in the UK, a lesbian group accused Stonewall, the gay-rights organisation, of discriminating against them. Stonewall had argued that biological men who identified as women could call themselves lesbians. The Lesbian Rights Alliance refused to accept this and consequently were accused by Stonewall of being transphobic. The Lesbian Rights Alliance countered that as Stonewall was discriminating against lesbian women, they must remove the "L" from their claim to represent LGBT people.

Confused? Our culture certainly is. When there is a clash between two groups, both of whom claim that they are being "true to themselves" and accusing the other of being in some way phobic, then what do we do? Who gets to be true to themselves and who is forced not to be?

The "Higher Truth"

All of us implicitly have a "higher truth" that we want people to conform to before we say that they can be "true to themselves". Yet, rather than scrabble around to define what that truth is, we can turn to the Bible and find, with great relief, this pure, timeless truth: our true identity is given to us by God, not discovered by us within.

The questions and inconsistencies drop away when we embrace the fact that God has told us what it means to be true to ourselves. Being true to ourselves *is* a good thing... but only if we are true to God's design of us. All of us need external validation. All of us appeal to a higher truth. We find these things in their fullest sense in God's verdict upon us as human beings made in his image.

We'll spend the next couple of chapters exploring what exactly this means. But it's worth remembering at this stage that a Christian has an even greater verdict upon them. As well as recognising the privilege of being made in the image of God, the Christian needs to keep hearing how God views them in Christ:

⁹ But you are a chosen people, a royal priesthood, a holy nation, God's special possession, that you may declare the praises of him who called you out of darkness into his wonderful light. ¹⁰ Once you were not a people, but now you are the people of God; once you had not received mercy, but now you have received mercy. (1 Peter 2 v 9-10)

The opinion that matters most is God's. And if you're a follower of Jesus, God says to you, *I have chosen you to be my special and treasured possession.* That's who you are.

Knowing this provides a solution to all the struggles and pressures that "be true to yourself" is trying to address.

Knowing this gives you the courage to be authentic. It means you're secure enough to be honest about what you're not good at, where you've messed up and how you need help—as well as confident when you've got something to contribute.

Knowing God's opinion gives you the strength to resist peer pressure—whether it's the temptation to have one too many drinks at a party or take part in a large-scale doping programme involving performance-enhancing drugs in sport.

Knowing that God approves of you means you won't be crushed by unfair criticism at work. You won't be in a permanent state of FOMO (fear of missing out) in your social life. Enjoying a meaningful relationship with God frees you to enjoy meaningful relationships with others. And knowing that his priority for your life is your holiness gives you a reliable yardstick against which to make decisions.

Knowing God's love for us will free us to be true to ourselves in the most fundamental of ways—true to our design. We're not made simply to listen to ourselves; we're made for glory! That's far more satisfying.

2. FINDING OURSELVES IN REFLECTING GOD

"What is mankind that you are mindful of them,
human beings that you care for them?
You have made them a little lower than the angels
and crowned them with glory and honour."
Psalm 8 v 4-5

Siri is a mine of useful information. (Have you ever tried asking, "Why are fire engines red?" Go on; try it.) But Siri is less useful on the more profound issues of life. This morning I tried asking, "Siri, what is the meaning of life?" The response was "Matt, you could mean a movie, or some people say it's chocolate". Not so helpful. I tried again: "Siri, what should I do with my life?" Answer: "Matt, I'm really not sure what to say".

What are we humans here for? How do we live a life that's worthwhile? In many ways, the "be true to yourself" philosophy is an attempt to answer that question—it reflects a good and distinctly human desire for meaning and satisfaction. It holds up the promise of a sense of worth... if only we can carve out and live out our true identity.

We all want a sense of meaning. But, boy, is it hard work creating one. By contrast, the loving Creator God says to us, *Stop trying to create meaning. I've given you a glorious one.*

Our restless striving can cease if we hold true to this: God has made us in his image to share his glory.

Meet the Glorious God

The glory of the Lord is the splendour and brilliance of all that he is. All of his attributes and his character constitute his glory: his power to achieve all things; his knowledge of all things past, present and future; his sovereign rule over all things; his wisdom, kindness, faithfulness and justice; his mercy, compassion, holiness and love. There's one word which sums all of this up: glorious.

The glory of God is like the splendour of the sun—our whole world is dependent upon it, but you cannot draw too close. It is breathtaking in its beauty and overwhelming in its goodness. But when God displays all that he is, it's just too much for a human to take in. In the Old Testament, God revealed his glory at Mount Sinai, and the people were overwhelmed and scared. God's glory dwelled in the temple, and no one could enter into the throne room or Most Holy Place. The glory of God is, in the true sense of the word, *awesome*.

Given how stunning God's glory is, the truth we find in Psalm 8 (and elsewhere in the Bible) should come as something of a surprise: rather than hold us at arm's length indefinitely, God has made us to enjoy his glory, to reveal his glory, to share his glory.

For the director of music. According to gittith.
A psalm of David.

¹ *LORD, our Lord,*
  how majestic is your name in all the earth!
 You have set your glory
  in the heavens.

² *Through the praise of children and infants*
  you have established a stronghold against your
  enemies,
  to silence the foe and the avenger.

³ *When I consider your heavens,*
  the work of your fingers,
 the moon and the stars,
  which you have set in place,

⁴ *what is mankind that you are mindful of them,*
  human beings that you care for them?

⁵ *You have made them a little lower than the angels*
  and crowned them with glory and honour.

⁶ *You made them rulers over the works of your hands;*
  you put everything under their feet:

⁷ *all flocks and herds,*
  and the animals of the wild,

⁸ *the birds in the sky,*
  and the fish in the sea,
  all that swim the paths of the seas.

⁹ *LORD, our Lord,*
  how majestic is your name in all the earth!

The main purpose of this psalm is to move us to worship God because of his creation, and, in particular, because of what we learn about the pinnacle of his creation—humanity. However, the psalm also shows us two important things about ourselves as we seek to "be true to ourselves". Quite simply, we're not gods... but we wear crowns. Holding those two things together is tricky, but essential.

We're Not Gods...

Consider the heavens, the work of God's fingers (v 3), the psalmist urges us. And we sure love to do that. In the UK, this is seen in our obsession with any nature documentary narrated by the naturalist David Attenborough. *Planet Earth 2* was the most-watched programme on the BBC's on-demand streaming service in 2016, and the following year its underwater equivalent, *Blue Planet 2*, was the most watched thing on TV overall. There aren't many TV shows that cross generations and can hold grandparents, parents, teenagers and toddlers alike in rapt attention as these did. We can't help but watch these kinds of programmes and say, "Wow. The variety of life in this world is amazing."

As Christians, we can go one step beyond that, and say, "Wow. God is amazing. Lord, I'm captivated by the work of your hands."

But according to this psalm, there's one more step we need to take in our thinking. When we gaze at the beauty, the power and the ingenuity of all God's creatures, we should naturally find ourselves thinking, "Wow—why does God

30

bother with me? Given there's so much life in the world, why are humans so special? Why does the Lord care *so much* for little old us?" Or as the psalmist puts it, "What is mankind that you are mindful of them?" (v 4).

God has given each human being an extraordinary status: he's made us just "a little lower than the angels", and so we are higher than anything else on this planet (v 5). Despite the fact that we share 95% of our DNA with a chimpanzee, 60% with a chicken, and even 50% with a banana, we are supreme among God's creatures. Why would the Lord care so much about us? Yet he does. Along with David (the psalmist, not Attenborough), we should wonder at that.

I observed this reaction one year on holiday. On the beach one day my son saw Jack Nowell. That name will have passed many of you by. But for a rugby-obsessed 13-year-old, the sight of an idol who has played for England and the British and Irish Lions was very exciting. My son follows Jack Nowell on social media and so quickly confirmed that it really was him, as Jack had updated his profile to say he was staying nearby.

Yet very quickly, great excitement turned to shyness and apprehension. Despite my encouragement to go and say hello and congratulate Jack on a great season, my son was too intimidated. So I wandered over to Jack, apologised for interrupting his ice-cream consumption and spoke to him myself. For the record, he is a super guy. He could not have been more friendly. After a couple of minutes he came over to my son and said, "Hi Nathan, we've not met, but I'm Jack. Shall we get a selfie together?" I thought my son might faint...

I could read the expression on his face: "Me? Jack Nowell came over and introduced himself to *me*? Asked for a selfie with *me*? I thought he would be annoyed, but he cares about *me*?"

It was a lovely moment. And it should also be our response before the Lord. *Me? Mankind? What are humans that the Lord should care so much for us?* (v 4). He has made us just a little lower than the angels. Wow. He has crowned us with glory and honour. Amazing.

... Although It Seems Appealing

But often, our response strays in a different direction.

Decades ago, as an undergraduate student, I remember being made to read John Stuart Mill's classic book *On Liberty*. At the time, the idea of reading a book of philosophy didn't excite me. Yet I remember reading, then underlining, and then copying out certain words: "Over himself, over his own body and mind, the individual is sovereign".

I thought those words were electric. They made me feel impressive, important and powerful. They meant that I was in total control of my own self—I loved the idea!

But it's not true. I am not sovereign over myself. The Lord is sovereign, and I belong to him. And so do you.

It's like this. You're reading a book that I wrote. I don't want to be crabby, but it's my work. You're not allowed to edit it or claim it as your own. If you did so, I would be entitled to take you to court. (However, I do have better things to do.)

Bulging heavily in my pocket is my wallet. (Actually, my wallet is invariably empty, but you get the idea.) The money in it is mine, as I earned it. You're not allowed to remove the money and say it's yours. We call that theft. If you steal the money from my wallet or bank account, the police might take you to court.

This is not complicated as an idea—if you make something, then you own it. God made us, and he owns us.

The assumption of the modern world is that we are sovereign—that each individual has the right to act independently and do what they want. Related to that is the belief that happiness only comes when we're free from any constraints upon us: free from want, from authority, from societal norms, from expectations. It's this belief that lies behind the old saying to "live and let live", and its more modern equivalent "You do you". To be happy, I must be free to choose where I live and what I do; free to love whoever I want and in whatever way I want; free from friends who drag me down or from family who place undue expectations on me. Essentially, I must be sovereign over all areas of my life—and to say otherwise is not just considered strange but, increasingly, immoral.

Yet Psalm 8 reminds us that we're not sovereign. We're owned by the true and living God. We don't create our identity and value. They are given to us. We're not gods. The Lord is the first, and we are his reflection. He is sound and we are echo. He is king and we are servants. We are image, not original—which means we can only understand what it is to be "human" after we have looked at God.

If we're more inspired and excited by reading John Stuart Mill (or whatever modern equivalent we find on upworthy.com) than contemplating our own smallness, it's likely that we've lost sight of how glorious God is, and, as we're about to see, how he shares that glory with us.

We're Not Gods... But We Wear Crowns

What a statement! "You have ... crowned [human beings] with glory and honour" (v 5). It's the same concept that we find in Genesis 1 when, after creating all of the other creatures, God says:

Let us make mankind in our image, in our likeness, so that they may rule over the fish in the sea and the birds in the sky, over the livestock and all the wild animals, and over all the creatures that move along the ground. (Genesis 1 v 26)

To be made in God's image = to be crowned with glory. Humanity is the finest of all of God's works. The almighty God, who dwells in unapproachable light, has revealed himself in creation, and the highest form of his revelation is… us. We do image him. We do reflect him. We *do* reveal him. We are uniquely privileged.

The God who speaks made beings who speak—from moving love songs to inspiring speeches. The God who creates made beings who can create—from architecture and apps to babies and blancmanges. The God who is relational made beings who are designed for relationships. To be "true to self"—to be who we *really* are—is determined by our relationship with the God in whose image we're made. After all, an image is just an image; it's not the real thing. You can have an original painting without a copy, but you can't have a copy without the original. We have extraordinary dignity *because God gave it to us*.

That means that every person has real, objective, magnificent value. There are no "ordinary people". There are no "mere mortals". We are made in God's image. That can be said of no other creature.

We'll think more about how that makes us relational beings in chapter 3, but the emphasis of Psalm 8 is that we reflect God's glory by ruling. He lets us rule for him; that shows exceptional trust and generosity. How extraordinary that God has created us to appreciate and make use of his creation. We get to explore and enjoy his world—to play in this theatre of his divine glory while knowing that, above all, we are the highest expression of God's glory in creation.

When travelling overseas, I've occasionally had generous friends who have said, "Here's the family car—take it for a few days to drive up the coast". That's real kindness and trust (especially since I'm used to driving on the *wrong* side of the road). Or, I can remember back 15 years ago, when the founding pastor of the church I serve said to me as a young man who had just turned 30, "I want you to take over Christ Church. I've seen it planted and established. You've been here and observed me—now I think you should take over." I felt a great sense of privilege, excitement... and nerves.

Now, God's creation is a far larger deal than a car or even one church. Yet we rule it under him—filling it with our families, ordering it through our work, dreaming up new uses for its resources. What a privilege!

The right and proper response is to praise the Lord for his majesty (v 9)—to praise him for the extraordinary privilege we have! We find our identity in worshipping this generous God. Our life's purpose is to enjoy him as we gratefully serve him in this world.

We're not gods... but we wear crowns.

To genuinely be "true to self", you need to be true to who you are as an image-bearer of God. You will only find a lasting sense of meaning in honouring the original of whom you are an image.

Tarnished Glory

And yet... the natural setting of the human heart is to reject what we've been given and chase after far less. We don't want to be a mirror; we want to shine in our own right, on our own terms.

The great irony is that if we exchange the glorious humility that the Lord has given us for an insignificant self-importance, we become far less. Our attempts at enlarging ourselves only leave us diminished. The pursuit of self-glorification turns out to be degrading.

One recent social-media flurry was caused when the British comedian David Baddiel posted a photo of his 13-year-old son sitting on a boulder on a stunning stretch of the rugged Cornish coastline. In this breathtaking setting, his son was hunched over his mobile phone. Baddiel wrote sarcastically, "Ezra, hypnotised and overawed as ever by the beauty of nature". His tweet went viral and was then met with replies of almost identical photos of children absorbed with their phones despite being in spectacular locations such as the Austrian Alps, Glacier Point in Yosemite National Park and Loch Doon in Scotland.

It seems daft to be so turned in on oneself when surrounded by a beauty which is so exhilarating. Yet that is precisely what humans do when we neglect the glory of God and seek to create our own crowns. We reject real glory and try to survive on the glory we eke out for ourselves.

In fact, we're worse. It's as if God puts us at Glacier Point, Yosemite or on top of the Alps, and invites us to enjoy a view that would lift us and put a smile on our faces—but we pull out a mirror and say, "I'd rather look at myself".

To reject the crown of glory that God has given us is to make ourselves less and to miss out. We will live diminished lives as we try to create a purpose for ourselves which is far inferior to the one God has given us.

We're not our own gods, but we have been crowned with glory.

Let's look at a couple of ways in which this makes a practical difference.

i. Human Dignity

Back in 1859, the same year that J.S. Mill was declaring, "Over himself, over his own body and mind, the individual is sovereign", Charles Darwin published *On the Origin of Species*. Christians will hold a variety of views on the role of evolution in human history, but one implication of Darwin's thinking is clearly a little disturbing. The full title of his book was *On the Origin of Species by Means of Natural Selection or the Preservation of Favoured Races in the Struggle for Life*.

Favoured races? Yes, Darwin thought some were superior to others. He wrote at the time, "The Western nations of Europe ... now so immeasurably surpass their former savage progenitors [that] the civilised races of man will almost certainly exterminate and replace the savage races through the world" (Charles Darwin, *The Descent of Man* Vol II, p 796-797). Darwin had no problem with European settlers wiping out indigenous people groups.

Now, I know very few people who hold to that view today. However, without a belief that God has created mankind in his image, it becomes difficult to come up with a clear answer to the question "Why is racism wrong?" Here's how the dialogue might run:

"Why is racism wrong?"

"Because all people are equal."

"Who says all people are equal? What if I think my race is superior to yours?"

"Well, the majority of the population think that people are equal."

"Maybe, but if the majority of the population were racist, does that mean that racism is right?"

"Er, well... you're wrong."

That's a well-intentioned but ultimately not very satisfactory basis for insisting that racism is wrong. By contrast, the Bible's answer is that all humans are made in God's image and therefore worthy of honour. In the Christian worldview there's an *inherent* dignity to humanity—but that's not the case if it's down to us to create our own meaning and purpose.

The result is that some secular voices instinctively say, "If you know your baby has Down syndrome, then you should abort it. They will have a poor quality of life." It's a tragic line of argument that angers me, but unless the quality of each and every human is considered inherently valuable, regardless of what they achieve for themselves or contribute to society—then why not? If we're not made in God's image, what answer do you give to the question "Why is racism wrong?"

ii. Personal Value

The same point can be made about individuals. When I was a schoolteacher, I was friends with a 50-year-old colleague who was single and lived a highly promiscuous lifestyle. We were pretty different but enjoyed each other's company. One summer I asked him how he intended to spend his long break. His reply stunned me. He told me he had to get to the gym every day and pick up a good tan without adding to his lines. He said, "The thing you have to remember is that for a man like me, when you lose your looks, you're a nobody".

It's sad to hear it put so starkly. Yet it's a view that's echoed in the fact that spending on beauty and grooming products continues to rise among all age groups of the population. Most acutely, Glamour magazine reports that, in the UK, young people aged 16-24 now use an average of 16 beauty products a day, worth £153 in total.

Why so much? Because when we reject the glory we're given, we will try to create our own. For many that will be in their physical appearance. Others seek this sense of value from the places they visit and can display on Instagram, and still others from their work or relationships. But all of it is shaky ground for finding our value.

How much time do you invest in your bodily appearance or in curating pictures for social media? What does that say about what makes you feel valuable?

Lasting Glory

Psalm 8 declares that human beings are "crowned ... with glory and honour" (Psalm 8 v 5). You may well read that and think, "Well, it doesn't *feel* like it". Sometimes it seems as if I can't control my garden, my dog or even my computer— so much for being one of God's rulers! Sometimes life is painful in the midst of suffering. Often life is just a bit disappointing. It looks anything but glorious.

That's because although God designed us for glory, humanity rejected his good plan back in the Garden of Eden. Our forebears failed to rule over creation as they should have, so now all of us have cracked crowns. To use the phrase of the theologian Francis Schaeffer, we are "glorious ruins". We continue to fail to image God in his world as we desperately try—and fail—to create our own glory.

But, of course, God's story does not end with our failure. Back in Genesis 1, God declared that mankind was "in [his] image". By contrast, "the Son is *the* image of the invisible God, the firstborn over all creation" (Colossians 1 v 15). Jesus is the Son of Man, and the one that Psalm 8 was ultimately looking to. Since his death, resurrection and ascension, there has been a man of flesh and blood sitting in glory upon his Father's throne, guaranteeing that we will join him there if we trust in him. Looks fade, jobs end, money runs out. It's terribly sad if you're holding on to a glory which fades so quickly. But this glory doesn't.

In Jesus we have a glory that lasts. You know those times when you're having a great time and you're aware of the moment? You're on holiday with some of your best friends, and it's brilliant. You're having good, unrushed time with family, and everyone is getting on without arguments. You're seeing something of staggering beauty or amazing skill. You're conscious of the moment and think, "I wish that this could last for ever". When we go to be with Jesus in eternal glory, it will.

Until then, the wonder of God's grace means that it is not "just" that we behold God's glory in creation and say "wow", but that he calls us to share it. We don't "just" see God's beauty; we're united with it. We don't "just" delight in Jesus; we become like him—believers "are being transformed into his image with ever-increasing glory" (2 Corinthians 3 v 18).

To be true to ourselves is not to search for or create our own identity and meaning. It is to know we have been given identity and meaning by our Creator.

You're not a god, but you do wear a crown. Enjoy it and praise the Lord who made you this way.

3. FINDING OURSELVES IN KNOWING OTHERS

> *"No man is an island,*
> *Entire of itself;*
> *Every man is a piece of the continent,*
> *A part of the main."*
> **John Donne**

John Donne's famous words express something that we all know, deep down: we need others. Of course, we might like the idea of *visiting* an island—most of us need a little "me time" now and then. But the idea of *living* on an island, alone, for ever? I'm yet to meet someone who actually wants that. We'd end up looking like Tom Hanks in the film *Castaway* (google-image it) and probably going a little mad. We don't want to be alone.

In fact, there's a growing body of evidence that shows that loneliness is incredibly damaging—and that it's on the rise in the West. One survey of 20,000 people found that 50% of Americans consider themselves to be lonely, with members of Generation Z (born between the mid-1990s and early 2000s) coming off worst. It's become such a source of anxiety in the UK that the government has now even appointed a Minister for Loneliness.

The reasons for this "loneliness epidemic" are many and various—but it's hard not to see a link of some kind between the growing culture of expressive individualism and rising rates of social isolation. After all, today's "cry of freedom" is that I create meaning for myself. I don't need other people's validation. To be true to myself, I look within; I follow my own feelings. In the words of former Apple CEO Steve Jobs at a Commencement Address at Stanford University, "Don't let the noise of others' opinions drown out your own inner voice".

It sounds liberating—but is it actually liveable? Clearly not for the 44% of Tinder users who use the dating app mainly as a "confidence boost". (It turns out that only 22% of the students in a recent survey said they used Tinder to "hook up"—most of the rest are looking for the sense of approval that comes from getting a match.[3]) Even if you're not on Tinder, I'm guessing that you know the kind of hit that comes from that notification signal every time you get a like on Instagram or a new message on WhatsApp. But this is a cotton-candy solution to a deep-seated hunger; we need meaningful relationships with others. We can't live without their approval.

There's also a sense in which we need others in order to understand ourselves. As the writer C.S. Lewis observed years ago in *The Four Loves*:

"As soon as we are fully conscious, we discover loneliness. We need others physically, emotionally, intellectually; we need them if we are to know anything, even ourselves."

Do you see what he's saying? We can only find ourselves in relationships with others. I can only know I'm an extrovert by spending time with others. I can only know what I think politically by debating with others. So the idea of self-fulfilment is a contradiction in terms. It turns out that we cannot be personally fulfilled without being relationally fulfilled.

Sacrifices Make Great Relationships

A further conundrum in the 21st century is that meaningful relationships involve sacrifices. I get on very well with my wife (you'll be pleased to hear!), but the relationship we share comes at the cost of independence. I give up freedom over how to spend money and time. I don't always choose who to spend time with or where we go to do that.

This reality comes into conflict with the "be true to yourself" philosophy. If being true to myself means following my own feelings and putting my own happiness and wellbeing first, I'll often find that comes at the expense of looking out for others.

Here's a little example: sometimes I'll hear people at church lamenting that they don't feel that they have good friends. Yet they'll also admit to bailing on people at the last minute because they "felt more like going home and chilling out". But the cost of great friendship is commitment; it's being there even when you don't want to be. You may be true to your feelings if you flake on someone, but if they were looking forward to meeting up, it means that you being true to self = being false to others. In a church setting, you may not feel like returning early from a weekend away to get back to an evening service, but your church friends would really like you to. Do your desires always trump those of your friends? So, which is most important: the freedom to be true to yourself or enjoying lasting relationships?

Wonderfully, in God's design we don't need to play these two things off against each other. In this chapter and the previous one, we're looking at what it means to be true to ourselves *as God has made us*, in his image. We can never fulfil ourselves; we need others. Yes, *need*. It's a much-overused word but appropriate here. God has made us for relationships, and we cannot function without them.

God Made Us for Others

In the beginning of the Bible, we're told that after making all of the creatures, God said:

> [26] *"Let us make mankind in our image, in our likeness, so that they may rule over the fish in the sea and the birds in the sky, over the livestock and all the wild animals, and over all the creatures that move along the ground."*

[27] So God created mankind in his own image,
in the image of God he created them;
male and female he created them.

[28] God blessed them and said to them, "Be fruitful and increase in number; fill the earth and subdue it. Rule over the fish in the sea and the birds in the sky and over every living creature that moves on the ground."

(Genesis 1 v 26-28)

There are two main elements to being in the image of God, and they are woven together in these verses:

1. We represent him by ruling (as we thought in chapter 2).

2. We relate like him.

Look closely at the lines of poetry:

In the image of God   *he created them*

Male and female   *he created them*

Can you see how the image of God is paralleled with male and female? There's a sense in which for humanity to be made in God's image human beings are made male and female. It is not that God is male and female. But he is three in one: Father, Son and Spirit. Each Person of the Trinity is different and cannot be equated as the same. Yet they are all equal, and God remains one.

In a similar sort of way, humanity is two in one: male and female (and if that's something you're not convinced of, we'll think more about gender in chapter 6). There is something about the sameness and difference of men and women that helps us understand God. There is something in a duality of the sexes that helps us know the plurality of Persons in God.

We learn that in the Trinity there is a mutual dependence, a capacity for relationship and difference that brings out the best in each other. This finds an echo in humanity. The "variety" is most obvious in male and female but is also true in all human relationships; we are all different, and we need one another's differences to flourish.

Or, to put it very simply, the living God is a loving community of Father, Son and Spirit—which means that humanity, made in his image, is meant for community too. There is a sense in which no one person on their own can reflect all that is meant by the image of God.

What does community life look like in the Trinity? We get a glimpse from Jesus in John's Gospel:

No one has ever seen God, but the one and only Son, who is himself God and is in the closest relationship with the Father, has made him known.   *(John 1 v 18)*

That's actually a very tricky verse to translate. Often the phrase "in the closest relationship with the Father" is translated as "at the Father's side". In the original Greek it literally says, "in the Father's breast".

What an intimate picture! I have to tell you that no one lies on my breast but my wife. My kids have done so in the past, but they would feel a little awkward doing so now they're older. I have some good friends, but none of them have that level of intimacy. Yet the Father and the Son go beyond "upon the breast" to "*within* the breast". This is how they lived in eternity past (although, given that at that point, neither the Father nor the Son had bodies, this must be some kind of metaphor). Or, as Jesus puts it in John 14 v 11, "I am in the Father and the Father is in me". That's weird to imagine spatially!

Perhaps think of it like this: with some people, the more you know, the less you like (let's be honest). But there are other relationships in which the more you get to know someone, the more you enjoy them—the more you love them. When that relationship grows in honesty and you can tell the other person everything, holding nothing back, and *still* they love you... that's truly wonderful. Not many relationships, even within marriage, reach that level of emotional nakedness with everything exposed. If you can have that level of honesty and know that the other person still loves you, it's priceless.

And that's what we're made for. We'll never quite know that Trinity-like level of relationship here on earth, not while we're still sinful. Yet we *are* made in the image of God. We're designed as humans to echo the relationships at the heart of the Trinity.

So, isolated individuals are incomplete. Human life can only reach its fulness in relationships with others. This is why there's an inner restlessness in all of us for love, affirmation and intimacy. We find that love in knowing God *and* in relationship with other people. Remember Jesus' definition of the greatest commandment? *Love God and love your neighbour.* So we need God, and we need neighbours. In the UK, medical research now shows that loneliness is more likely to kill you than obesity—lonely people are twice as likely to die prematurely as those who don't feel isolated. The Bible says, *Don't be surprised.*

I can think of some single friends who have told me, "I don't care about sexual intercourse. I can live without that. It's a committed intimate nurturing relationship that I desire."

To which I think our response must be: "Of course you desire that!" The Bible makes us expect it.

A desire for deep relationship is hardwired into our souls. We're made with a restless quest for intimacy with God and with others. Yet this sense of incompleteness in all of us is NOT, in the Bible, fulfilled by romantic relationships or even marriage. That may be one place to find intimacy, but it is not the only place. And I would suggest, it's not necessarily the main place.

Ultimately, intimacy should be found in the family of God. Our churches need to be the kind of places that the New Testament expects them to be—places where deep friendships can be formed, where people are committed to each other and know they're cared for. This goes beyond the cheap and distant boost of a social-media hit; this is something deeper and more meaningful. It will take time, commitment and honesty (as we'll think about in chapter 8).

Working with Others Means We Can Rule the World

God has made us for intimacy—that's a wonderful truth that helps explain many of our longings for relationship. But remember, there are two main elements of being made in the image of God: to represent him and to relate like him. It's unhelpful to pull these too far apart. Instead, we need to hold all of Genesis 1 v 26-28 together. Being created in God's image (male and female) in verse 27 is surrounded by the command to rule in verses 26 and 28. God created us male and female in order to help us rule.

There's a similar pattern in Genesis 2:

> [15] *The LORD God took the man and put him in the Garden of Eden to work it and take care of it.* [16] *And the LORD God commanded the man, "You are free to eat from any tree in the garden;* [17] *but you must not eat from the tree of the knowledge of good and evil, for when you eat from it you will certainly die."* [18] *The LORD God said, "It is not good for the man to be alone. I will make a helper suitable for him."*
> *(Genesis 2 v 15-18)*

Adam is given his task in verse 15, and a command in verses 16-17, before the LORD makes the observation in verse 18 that it's not good for the man to be alone. Notice how it's God who says this. It's not Adam who pipes up,

I'm feeling a little lonely here, Lord. Rather it's the Lord God who says that the man requires a helper. It's not that he's lonely but that he is unable to rule on his own.

So the Lord resolves to create one who is, literally, "according to the opposite to" the man—or, more simply, a "helper", a "complement-er"—in order to make Adam able to do more than he could before. Now, there's a point to be made about two sexes here: even secular social studies say that, in general, men and women view the world differently—the two sexes are equal but different. Yet the larger point is that we need others. We simply cannot function—cannot "rule" our lives—on our own. So when a single friend tells us they're longing for a close relationship with someone they can rely on—someone who will help them navigate life through all its ups and downs—Genesis 1 and 2 tell us that's right. This job of ruling is meant to be done as a team.

But again, marriage is not the only team. In fact, Adam and Eve's relationship isn't just the first marriage; it's the first church—a gathering of God's people united in living for him. For believers today, living after Christ's resurrection but before his return, ruling the earth isn't only about putting men and women together to make babies; it's also about coming together as men and women to make disciples. And gender isn't the only way in which we're different. When you get to the New Testament, one of the most common ways of referring to a church community is as a body—all the parts need one another and no one part can carry out all the tasks on its own (see, for example, 1 Corinthians 12 v 12-31). We've got different gifts with which to serve each other. God has designed it so that we're interdependent.

I was struck by this at a recent guest event at church. I stood up and spoke for a few minutes. However, someone else in the church family had designed attractive graphics on handouts; someone else had decorated the room according to the relevant theme; some musicians provided music; a gang of people prepared food and another team served it; while yet another group cleared up at the end. It turned out to be a great evening because people were generous with their time; there's no way one person or even a handful could have made it happen.

Intimacy Comes from Giving Yourself

Intimacy: noun. Close familiarity or friendship.

God has made us with a mutual need for other people. Humans are created for relationships of dependence through difference. So any sensible attempt to be true to ourselves will require cultivating those kind of relationships. How do we do that?

The apostle John tells us that it is not romance that we need. It is sacrificial love within the church family.

⁷ Dear friends, let us love one another, for love comes from God. Everyone who loves has been born of God and knows

God. [8] Whoever does not love does not know God, because God is love. [9] This is how God showed his love among us: he sent his one and only Son into the world that we might live through him. [10] This is love: not that we loved God, but that he loved us and sent his Son as an atoning sacrifice for our sins. [11] Dear friends, since God so loved us, we also ought to love one another. (1 John 4 v 7-11)

A quick search of over 50 wedding sermons that I've given reveals 1 John 4 to be the most popular passage for couples to pick. Yet these verses, in common with many other great passages in the Bible on human love, are not about romantic love in a marriage—they're about love within a church family. Some people will assume that if they never marry, then they've been denied an intimacy essential for life. That's not true.

This is not a passage about sex or marriage, although it has lots to say to those subjects. It is primarily about showing one another a love defined by Jesus: self-giving love. Sacrificial love. *That's* the love that Jesus has shown humanity. *That's* the love we're meant to show others.

Yet if we're seeking self-fulfilment by being true to ourselves, we're left with some questions: Why would I sacrifice if it stops me doing what I desire? Why would I love you when I need to place my own feelings first? Why would I give when I get nothing back?

But sacrificial love is wonderful. After all, it is essential to the gospel message that Jesus Christ sacrificed himself in place of undeserving sinners like me and you. When we show this kind of sacrificial love for others, it is not necessarily a love that we feel. It's not always a love that is aroused in us by someone else. It's a resolve to love even when it hurts; even when I don't want to; even when I would desire to choose something else.

Parents of small children tend to find this easiest to understand. When you have a newborn, you give up sleep, convenience and comfort for the baby. For six weeks, you don't even get a smile in return! Yet most parents would testify to joy in this—you can laugh as you clear up a dirty nappy or be patient when your baby vomits on you.

We find it harder to show the same kind of self-giving love to an adult as we expect so much more of them. But that is the sort of love we're meant to display and that we're *made* to display: a self-giving, patient, kind, other-person-centred love. A love that images God's love within the Trinity.

As we pursue this, we'll find that we can't genuinely have "Be true to yourself" without "Love your neighbour"—and that living this way is so satisfying. I can think of one young woman who arrived at our church feeling fairly broken from a damaged relationship in the past. She was adamant that from now on she "needed to be more selfish"—to "care less about other people's views and more about my own". She carried on in that frame of mind for a while, but it was only when she got involved in teaching one of the children's groups on Sundays that she really started to recover. She was part of a team that looked out for one another and that needed one another each week for things to work. She found great pleasure in giving out to the children, and then being invited in to join the families for lunch afterwards, and then eventually into the mess of their everyday lives. It was lovely to see.

Humans are made in the image of God for relationship—with him and with others. We crave love. If we reject the Lord (or as Christians neglect him), then it creates a desperate need for affirmation within us. But when we come to him, his Spirit gives us the resources we need to give out to others in sacrificial love.

And as we do so, we'll discover the surprising yet satisfying payback that God has woven into his design: that to be true to one another is to be true to ourselves.

4. FINDING OURSELVES IN SEEING CHRIST

*"Amazing grace, how sweet the sound that
saved a wretch like me."*
John Newton

The bestselling memoir *Eat, Pray, Love* tells the story of Elizabeth Gilbert's journey of self-discovery and spiritual exploration following a difficult divorce. After travelling around Italy, India and Indonesia, she arrives at this philosophy: "God dwells within you as yourself, exactly the way you are" (Elizabeth Gilbert, *Eat, Pray, Love*, chapter 64). The fact that the book has sold over 12 million copies, and has since been made into a film, shows that this is a philosophy that is very much in tune with the modern ear.

In some ways it's grasping at the truth—there is something God-like about us. We've seen in the last two chapters that we're made in the image of God. This gives us a wonderful dignity and a basis for satisfying relationships. Yet we're merely mirrors—it's *who we reflect* that makes us special.

If you take out the reflective glass, then, without the image of the glorious God filling our "frame", we're left with something woefully uninspiring.

Yet this is precisely what our modern culture tries to do. Our society has increasingly rejected the idea of a creator and so looks within to find meaning. To caricature this for the sake of simplicity, here are our unexamined assumptions:

Q: What shall I worship?

A: Well, if there's no God, then... me.

Q: Who shall I love?

A: Me.

In rejecting God, many in the modern West have turned to an alternative "gospel"—by that, I mean a truth which people look to for happiness: a big philosophy to live by. And one of the biggest "gospels" our culture sells us is the gospel of self-esteem: "Look within to find out who you are: what you find is wonderful".

The Gospel of Self-esteem

Most of us are familiar with the concept of self-esteem. It describes the way that someone thinks about themselves, and the worth and value they ascribe to their person. High self-esteem is assumed to be desirable: people who possess this are confident, secure, trusting and resilient. Low self-esteem can manifest in self-criticism, pessimism or an excessive sense of guilt or need to please others. The "gospel" of self-esteem says that the way to be happy is to esteem yourself more highly. In other words, *love yourself*.

Christians can easily slip into these assumptions because they're nearly all helpful. Confidence, security and resilience are good things that we like. Excessive guilt and a slavish need to please others are unpleasant things that we dislike. So, the gospel of self-esteem sounds great!

In contrast, when we first encounter the biblical gospel, it might sound a little, well... miserable. At my church we sing, to a modern tune, Elizabeth Clephane's hymn "Beneath the cross of Jesus". I think that its picture of the cross as an oasis that we need in the desert of life is a very lovely one. But what do you think of the last two verses?

Upon that cross of Jesus,
Mine eye at times can see
The very dying form of one
Who suffered there for me;
And from my smitten heart, with tears,
Two wonders I confess:
The wonders of his glorious love
And my own worthlessness.

I take, O cross, thy shadow
For my abiding place;
I ask no other sunshine than
The sunshine of his face:
Content to let the world go by,

To know no gain nor loss,
My sinful self my only shame,
My glory all the cross.

So on a Sunday we gather several hundred people together to sing that we are worthless and ashamed of ourselves. What do you make of that?! And it's not that my church is a particularly gloomy one—if you've ever sung "Amazing Grace", you've sung these words: "Amazing grace, how sweet the sound that saved a wretch like me".

Do you believe that you are wretched? That doesn't sound good for self-esteem either!

But when we properly understand it, the gospel of Christ offers us the security, confidence and resilience that we really want and need. We can only be true to ourselves if we are honest. The true gospel compels us to accept that we're made in the image of God, but, because of our sins and flaws, we need to be redeemed into the image of Christ. He has made us lovely. It's not something we naturally are, but something we have been given.

Are We Always Wonderful?

This is a truth we see repeated throughout the Scriptures. The Lord wants his people to recognise their natural failure so that they rejoice at their identity in Christ.

Let's start in the Old Testament, where the prophet Ezekiel spoke about a time when God's people would be transformed by his Spirit—a promise that was fulfilled in the New Testament era.

But notice this: through Ezekiel, God tells his people that *after* they have been saved, they'll be ashamed.

Then you will remember your evil ways and wicked deeds, and you will loathe yourselves for your sins and detestable practices. I want you to know that I am not doing this for your sake, declares the Sovereign LORD. Be ashamed and disgraced for your conduct, people of Israel!

(Ezekiel 36 v 31-32)

So after the death and resurrection of Jesus and the outpouring of the Spirit (which Ezekiel points forward to), believers will "loathe" themselves because of their sin.

Similarly, at the end of the book of Job, after being addressed by the Lord, Job can say:

My ears had heard of you but now my eyes have seen you. Therefore I despise myself and repent in dust and ashes.

(Job 42 v 5-6)

It's at this point in the narrative that the Lord blesses Job more richly than he had ever been blessed—precisely when he despised himself, yet had a glorious view of God.

When we reach the New Testament, it doesn't speak of self-love as a good thing. When Paul talks about terrible times to come in Christian history, here is how he describes them:

> *But mark this: there will be terrible times in the last*
> *days. People will be lovers of themselves, lovers of money,*
> *boastful, proud, abusive, disobedient to their parents,*
> *ungrateful, unholy.*   *(2 Timothy 3 v 1-2)*

A sign of terrible times is that people will be "lovers of themselves". Moreover, when Paul writes to the proud, boastful Corinthian church, who fail to love one another, he does not put the problem down to low self-esteem. Rather he says:

> *If I speak in the tongues of men or of angels, but do not*
> *have love, I am only a resounding gong or a clanging cymbal.*
> *If I have the gift of prophecy and can fathom all mysteries*
> *and all knowledge, and if I have a faith that can move*
> *mountains, but do not have love, I am nothing.*
>   *(1 Corinthians 13 v 1-2)*

Paul states clearly that even if you have all sorts of wonderful gifts, without love for others you are "nothing". Not a great morale boost! These Christians need to stop loving themselves and love others.

Do you see the Bible's overall picture? We're not meant to look within and say "lovely". We're not meant to pursue self-love—that would be, in Paul's words, "terrible". Being true to ourselves in any realistic way involves looking at our character and recognising that we're flawed. In contrast with God's design for us, we're fallen. In that sense, it's entirely right that we have a negative *moral* self-image. That is not unhealthy. It's honest. When we stand before the holy God, we are *moral* failures. We are not worthy of love from God or from ourselves!

But, I *Am* Special...

I wonder if the biblical way of describing Christians jarred a little with you. "Yes," you say, "I know the Bible has stuff about people being 'miserable sinners', but... I'm not *that* bad really. And what about that bit where we're meant to love our neighbours as ourselves? Surely that implies a bit of self-love is necessary."

Well, please bear in mind our tendency towards "Better than average" syndrome, which I mentioned in chapter 1: 98% of us think we're nicer than average! By nature, we are all like unscrupulous real estate agents. You know the kind? When they say, "Some work needed", they mean, "It's about to fall down". When they say, "Cosy", they mean, "A human cannot stand up in this". When they say, "It's an up-and-coming area", they mean, "When you exit your front door, run".

We're the same with our character. When we're asked, "Are you a kind person?" we reach for the estate agent's guide to putting the best possible spin on things. We deceive ourselves.

Part of this comes down to the culture that we're swimming in every day. The gospel of self-esteem has gradually been taking over Western culture for years, so that now we barely notice the assumptions behind it.

Back in 1931, the philosopher Ayn Rand wrote these words as part of a short novel, *Anthem*:

"I am done with the monster of 'we', the world of serfdom, of plunder, of misery, falsehood, shame. And now I see the face of a god, and I raise this god over the earth, this god whom men have sought since men came into being, this god who will grant them joy and peace and pride.

"This god, this one word: I." (Ayn Rand, Anthem, part 11)

In other words, "we" is a monster; "I" is a God. Rand is less well known in the UK, but in the US, one poll that asked which book had had the largest influence on the respondent's life, rated her novel *Atlas Shrugged* second only to the Bible. Her economic views shaped the policy of Alan Greenspan, who ran the Federal Reserve in the USA for 30 years, as well as Margaret Thatcher's view on shrinking the state and encouraging individual responsibility. So, as regards the economy, we've been told for decades that it is virtuous to place the needs of individuals above the group. Rand has persuaded many that "We" is a monster, but "I" is a god.

Yet it was during the 1980s that the popularity of the idea that self-esteem is important for mental health rocketed. Social historians point to a California State task force on self-esteem as being a massive turning point in the mainstream acceptance of this idea. But perhaps a more important moment was in 1990, when Oprah Winfrey presented a prime-time special all about self-esteem and how it would be part of one of the most significant movements of the following years. And it certainly has been.

The idea that self-esteem needs continual promotion is now implemented in teaching from the earliest age. A nursery-school teacher at our church told me that during her training, she was encouraged to get the children (aged 3-5) to sing, to the tune of "Frére Jacques":

"I am special
I am special
Look at me; you will see
Someone very special
Someone very special
Because it's me
Because it's me"

Similarly, in the UK there was a widely reported story about Barrowford Primary School (for ages 4-11) in Lancashire. When they received their exam results in 2014, all 10-11-year-olds were sent a sweet letter telling them that...

"These tests do not always assess all of what it is that makes
each of you special and unique ... they do not know that your
laughter can brighten the dreariest day." (Quoted in Will
Storr, Selfie, p 218-219)

As the letter went viral, the headteacher revealed more about school policy. Teachers were told never to raise their voices with misbehaving children, but to tell them that "they are wonderful but making a mistake". There were no fixed break times or lunchtimes as the children decided when they wanted a break themselves. The head commented that no matter what they did, pupils were to be treated with "unconditional positive regard".

This heart-warming story was met with realism the following year when the school was inspected by government body OFSTED and found to be "inadequate". The head came under pressure to resign for enforcing a policy that did not work.

This focus on self-esteem is not limited to children. High self-esteem is also viewed as the route to success at work. In a recent sermon, a colleague quoted from Robert Greene's bestselling book *The 48 Laws of Power*. The contents list alone includes such "gems" as these:

- "Court attention at all costs. Never let yourself be lost in the crowd or buried in oblivion. Stand out! Make yourself a magnet of attention by appearing larger, more colourful, more mysterious than the bland masses."

- "Act like a king to be treated like one."

- "Do not commit to anyone or a cause but yourself."

- "Keep your hands clean. Conceal your mistakes, have a scapegoat around to blame."

The whole thesis of the book is *Act as if you're really important. Believe in yourself and never doubt.* It's a message you'll find repeated in countless self-help books, advice columns and lifestyle magazines.

This is the ocean of self-esteem that we swim in every day. And while that list of quotes may sound particularly outrageous, all of us can buy into a more subtle version of this view, probably without realising it. My teenage son had to give a public speech last night, and he was really nervous. My lazy brain almost said out loud to him, "You can do it; just have more self-belief", until I paused and thought, "Hold on, Matt. This is *precisely* what you're writing about." Happily, what emerged from my mouth was more balanced: "You've done this before, and it went fine. Let's pray and ask God to help you do it again."

It's so easy to drift with the assumption that a self-esteem boost is precisely what we all need. So how can we tell if we've been taken in? Consider this: when someone challenges you for something unkind or aggressive that you've said, is it your default to say...

a. "Oh come on, everyone was thinking it. Besides, you were far meaner last week, and it's not as bad as what he said" (and so you protect yourself by making a comparison). Or...

b. "You're right; sometimes my speech reveals that I'm not as nice as I like to think."

Admittedly that's a conversation painted in caricature— but which way do you naturally lean?

Or what about before a job interview? If you're feeling particularly nervous, what is your inner monologue?

a. "You're a champion. You deserve this. Pull yourself together and show them who is epic." Or...

b. "Lord, help me give an honest and good account of myself. I think I have the right experience and qualifications for this job, so help me to show the interviewers that I would be a great person for them to employ. If there is someone better equipped for the role, so be it. In that case, you have other plans for me."

Again, forgive the caricatures—but which way do you tend to lean? Might it be that in such moments you're repeating the gospel of self-esteem to yourself rather than a biblical view?

But We Are Given Beauty!

The Bible is clear that we are not naturally lovely... but we are given beauty. We are not naturally righteous... but we are given righteousness. We are not naturally clean... but when we're washed clean by the blood of Jesus, then we are perfect in God's sight. We are not naturally special inside... but we become God's special people.

Some of us find it easy to accept the first half of those sentences, but very difficult to believe the second half. (This will leave us no better off in the long term than the gospel of self-esteem.) Yet the gospel of Christ gives us both—or rather, it gives us "but". Look at these wonderful Bible BUTs, showing what we ourselves lack but what we've been given:

*Remember that at that time you were separate from Christ, excluded from citizenship in Israel and foreigners to the covenants of the promise, without hope and without God in the world. **But now** in Christ Jesus you who once were far away have been brought near by the blood of Christ.*
(Ephesians 2 v 12-13)

*All of us also lived among them at one time, gratifying the cravings of our flesh and following its desires and thoughts. Like the rest, we were by nature deserving of wrath. **But** because of his great love for us, God, who is rich in mercy, made us alive with Christ even when we were dead in transgressions—it is by grace you have been saved.*
(Ephesians 2 v 3-5)

*For you were once darkness, **but now** you are light in the Lord. Live as children of light.* *(Ephesians 5 v 8)*

*Once you were alienated from God and were enemies in your minds because of your evil behaviour. **But now** he has reconciled you by Christ's physical body through death to present you holy in his sight, without blemish and free from accusation.* *(Colossians 1 v 21-22)*

*Once you were not a people, **but now** you are the people of God; once you had not received mercy, but now you have received mercy.* *(1 Peter 2 v 10)*

*For "you were like sheep going astray," **but now** you have returned to the Shepherd and Overseer of your souls.*

(1 Peter 2 v 25)

"But" really is a wonderful word when it gets us out of trouble! Yet accepting all this is deeply humbling. In fact, there's something within us that is sometimes even tempted to resent it, or, at least, tempted to begin to think and act as if it's not true. We secretly think that we're pretty good assets for God's team. We want to look as if we have it all together. We don't want to be seen to fail. We'd rather be beautiful in and of ourselves. But we have to face reality—we're not. Yet we have been given a beauty that can never be lost.

Perhaps it's easier to think in these terms: a little while ago, while staying overseas, I had a problem with my credit card. It didn't work, and I had no cash left. I was financially exposed! Happily, someone I barely knew but with whom I was staying declared, "No problem; I'll give you my card for a couple of days. Here it is, and the pin is ####." It was fantastically kind and a bit of a life-saver.

Imagine if I'd have turned around and petulantly declared, "I don't want *your* money. I want *my own* money." That would have been ungrateful and would also have meant shooting myself in the foot. I needed to face reality. I had no money, but someone was giving me their bank card. So I didn't resist!

Similarly, a little reflection tells us that, actually, it's far better to be given moral beauty than to have to look inwards for it, because the moral beauty that Jesus gives us can never be lost and will never vary. It doesn't have good days and bad days. It doesn't get hangry or overtired. His moral beauty is constant—so we are always valuable.

There is wonderful comfort in the fact that even on our worst days, we are still loved because of Christ. There is more grace in Jesus than there is sin in you. You can't out-sin his mercy and so become ugly again! No matter how morally wretched we've been (and know we've been), we are still clothed in Christ's righteousness and beauty.

Remember that hymn? "My sinful self my only shame, my glory all the cross." When I'm honest and confess my sin, I'm ashamed of who I am. When I consider what Christ has done for me, then I'm thrilled with the cross—it's my glory! I know that my identity is found in being united to Jesus, and I'm delighted with the person Christ has made me. I can still hate the sin I commit while delighting in the fact that God loves me because I'm washed clean by Christ.

This allows us to be honest with ourselves and say, "My motives are always mixed, and sometimes I think and act in ways that are awful. And yet... despite who I am, I am still loved by God as my Father because of Jesus Christ."

Thinking this way means we can have confidence and resilience, alongside a healthy and appropriate guilt when we do wrong, and a suitable but not excessive concern for what others think.

When my temper flares up in front others I'll admit that I was never as nice as I thought. But Jesus has taken my shame.

When my sexual sin is exposed, I'll admit that I am not as moral as I like to pretend. But Jesus has washed me clean.

When I break my promises, I'll admit that I am not as good a friend as I make out. But Jesus is always faithful and has paid for my faithlessness.

So, which is healthier? The "gospel" of self-love, which is introspective and cannot bear to be honest about what is wrong, or the biblical gospel, which recognises that you're deeply flawed and yet even more deeply loved by Jesus?

Worldly self-love demands that you look within and find beauty. The gospel says that when you look within and find there's filth mixed in with the good, you don't have to pretend. You can acknowledge the truth and know you're loved by a greater judge than yourself.

This, then, is the self to whom we must be true: we are made in God's image to rule and relate; we are ruined by sin but restored in Christ.

Jesus invites us to stop looking in and, instead, look at him. Look at how wonderful he is—how loved he is by God the Father—and remember that if you're united to him by faith, then he shares this beauty with you. What's not to love?

5. IDENTITY:
CERTAINTY › SELF-CREATION

*"In a time of universal deceit, telling the truth is a
revolutionary act."*
George Orwell

The other day we watched the teen movie *The Maze Runner*
as a family. At the beginning you see a boy waking up
in a new place. He has no idea of his name or where he is.
He doesn't know what his skills are, who is on his side or
who wants to kill him. So, understandably, he freaks out!
The whole situation leaves him feeling confused, scared
and anxious. Eventually, as the movie rolls on, he discovers
that his name is Thomas and that he's been given the job of
solving the maze. There's great relief in remembering who
he is and what he's meant to do!

There's a sense in which this is a parable for our times.
When you reject your God-given identity—as a human
being made in God's image—then you have to construct
one for yourself. In one sense that sounds liberating:
you're free to be who you want to be, to experiment and

to grow. But in fact it proves to be exhausting. We have almost limitless options, but that can leave us confused, and we aimlessly drift on a quest of self-discovery.

This phenomenon shouldn't surprise us. It might be the spirit of the age, but it's not particularly modern. In a sense it's the spirit of *every* age. Paul described this mindset nearly 2,000 years ago, in Romans 1:

[21] *For although [people] knew God, they neither glorified him as God nor gave thanks to him, but their thinking became futile and their foolish hearts were darkened.* [22] *Although they claimed to be wise, they became fools* [23] *and exchanged the glory of the immortal God for images made to look like a mortal human being and birds and animals and reptiles.*

[24] *Therefore God gave them over in the sinful desires of their hearts to sexual impurity for the degrading of their bodies with one another.* [25] *They exchanged the truth about God for a lie, and worshipped and served created things rather than the Creator—who is for ever praised. Amen.*

(Romans 1 v 21-25)

Even a brief look at modern culture brings home how timelessly true these words in Romans 1 are. When we exchange the truth about God for a lie, then we worship created things. But it's a tragic exchange. We swap "the glory of the immortal God" for images. It's far worse than trading a priceless Van Gogh painting for a cheap postcard print of the same scene; it's worse than trading a mountaintop view for a child's graffiti on a garage door.

Our culture is swapping the all-satisfying, glorious truth that we are made in the image of a Creator God for the lie that we will be happier worshipping ourselves.

The Gospel of Self-creation

In the last chapter we looked at "the gospel of self-esteem": the idea that true happiness and fulfilment are found in loving myself. In this chapter we're going to move on a step further and think about a connected philosophy: the idea that not only should I *love* who I am but that I have the freedom to *define* who I am; and that, as such, any restriction on that freedom is a restriction on my happiness. We'll call this "the gospel of self-creation".

Although it's helpful to distinguish this from *mere* self-esteem, there's also a sense in which this second idea of self-creation has grown out of the first. The gospel of self-creation says, "Look within and see what you find. Discover who you are inside, and then conform what's around you on the outside in line with that. Only then can you be happy."

But as with all false gospels, when we start to pick away at the thinking behind our culture's philosophy of self-creation, things quickly start to unravel into a tangled heap of questions. So that's what we're going to pause to do in this chapter.

It's worth saying, though, that this discussion will touch on realities that for many people are deeply personal and often painful; that may well be the case for you. While this chapter takes on the broader cultural "logic", I want to say here that none of these issues are *only* about logic. They're about *people*—people with immense dignity and worth because they're made in God's image. The next chapter will deal with some of these questions on a more personal level.

Who Can Self-define?

One area of confusion in our culture is over which areas are open to self-definition, and which are not.

Take two high-profile individuals who wanted to self-define. Back in 2015, Caitlyn Jenner—known until then as Olympic athlete Bruce Jenner—transitioned from a man to a woman, saying, "I am a woman ... I was not genetically born that way ... But I still identify as a woman." This was met with huge support and media celebration.

Yet shortly afterwards, Rachel Dolezal (a white woman) hit the headlines when it was discovered that she was running a local branch of the National Association for the Advancement of Colored People, despite having two Caucasian parents. Dolezal insisted that she identified as black. She said, "White isn't a race; it's a state of mind." This was met with outrage and vitriol. She lost her job and was hounded for months on social media. One commentator wrote, "Transgender activists transition out of medical necessity. Dolezal's transition to black is surrounded by layers of deception" (Decca Aitkenhead, *The Guardian*, 25 Feb 17).

Pause and think about that statement. Why does a man feeling like a woman mean that transitioning is a medical necessity, but feeling and defining yourself as black is shrouded in layers of deception? How do you decide which feelings are legitimate—and should be acted on—and which are not? Why was Dolezal denied the freedom to self-define?

I don't ask these questions aggressively but in confusion. They highlight the fact that when we reject God's definition of who we are, life becomes complicated. In our current cultural moment, one person is affirmed for defining themself by how they feel, but another is told that how they feel is irrelevant. So which is it?

However, the furore surrounding Rachel Dolezal occurred back in 2015, and it seems that the culture has changed even since then. In the UK, theatre director Anthony Ekundayo Lennon identifies as mixed race despite, by his own admission, not being so genetically. As a consequence, in 2018 he was awarded a two-year training programme as part of an Arts Council grant of £400,000 reserved for people from black and minority ethnic backgrounds. Both his parents are white, but he describes himself as "African born-again" and says he always felt out of place in his family when he was growing up. Is it ok for a white man to benefit from a grant intended to help improve diversity in UK theatres? The media reaction to the story seemed divided.

Pause and ask yourself what you think: should someone be able to self-define their race?

Yet in other areas, self-identifying is viewed as unacceptable. Emile Ratelband is the Dutch "television personality" who applied to have his legal age changed from 69 to 49 in order to be able to a buy a new house and receive more positive responses on Tinder. He built his case on the fact that his doctor had told him that he had the body of a 40-something, and, as he put it, "We live in a time when you can change your name and change your gender. Why can't I decide my own age?"[4]

His application was rejected by the court, but essentially only because it was too difficult to implement. The ruling said, "Amending his date of birth would have a variety of undesirable legal and societal implications" (*The Independent*, 04 Dec 18).

Pause and ask yourself what you think: should someone be able to self-define their age?

Whose Right Wins?

It's not just the question of which areas should be open to self-definition that is subject to confusion. There's also the question of what happens when the freedom for some to self-create comes into conflict with the right of protection for others.

Trevor Phillips chaired the UK Equalities and Human Rights Commission from 2006 to 2012. He was tasked with protecting equality across nine grounds: age, disability, gender, race, religion, maternity, marriage, sexual orientation and gender reassignment. These nine areas are protected characteristics in UK law.

However, Phillips is now publicly arguing that the proposed movement to self-declaration of gender makes a mockery of Britain's decades-long struggle for fairness. The proposal is that, rather than continue the current system, where someone requires a medical diagnosis and a two-year period of living in their acquired identity before they can legally change gender, those seeking to transition should simply be allowed to self-declare, meaning that someone born a man could declare himself to be a woman and immediately have the right to enter spaces reserved for women. Phillips states that the cases of women in prisons being sexually assaulted by "women with penises" must give us pause for thought about whether this is wise (*The Times*, 22 Oct 18).

He argues that gender pay gap reporting, which aims to close the gap in pay between men and women, will become meaningless if it can become obscured by an easy fix in the paperwork, as will race-gap reporting. Phillips insists that this "makes a mockery of the struggle for equality".

Similarly, tennis player Martina Navratilova recently came under fire on Twitter. You might have thought that someone who had campaigned for 40 years for LGBT rights and had done so much for female equality in sport would be somewhat bulletproof in this regard. Yet she was assailed by people calling her transphobic after she had tweeted, "You can't just proclaim yourself female and then compete against women. There must be some standards."

Doesn't that seem like a reasonable viewpoint? That there need to be some agreed standards? Yet Navratilova describes the response she received as "bullying tweets like incoming fire" and also criticised the "tyranny" of the trans activists who assailed her—refusing to engage and merely denouncing her (*The Independent*, 17 Feb 19). It's not just Christian pastors like me who are concerned about how these kinds of debates are being shut down. In the current climate there are not too many like Phillips or Navratilova, who are willing to ask what is really quite a reasonable question, when they know the response will be outrage.

Pause and ask yourself what you think: should someone be able to self-define their gender?

An Objective Word from God

Perhaps, by now, this catalogue of examples has wound you up and you're thinking: "Even if the right to self-define is misused by some, that doesn't mean that self-definition itself is wrong. Abuse of a freedom by the few should not mean that it's withdrawn from the many." Yet it's also worth bearing in mind that the negative examples I've cited are not just cases of a few lone individuals. They have the support of thousands of people behind them (as well as equal or larger numbers of those who are bewildered by their claims).

My main aim is simply to point out the current inconsistency in modern thought. People insist that self-identifying is ok for some protected characteristics but not for others. Well, that seems arbitrary. Some of us will know and agree with people who want to redefine their "assigned" gender, or we may feel that way ourselves; yet we don't automatically agree that people should be able to redefine their race. Perhaps it's vice versa.

Our society has become increasingly disorientated on these issues because, when our objective, God-given identity is abandoned, then the issue of what it means to be a human is confused. Reality is being obscured so that race, gender, and age are all coming to be described as fluid. This fluidity is presented as marvellous progress.

The resulting minefield of human-rights ambiguities, and questions over who is allowed to say what, is bewildering. Conversation is shut down because of bullying outrage, and so most people are scared to say, "I'm not sure about this".

Many of us now have a default sympathy for any minority group, which is a good thing. It's right to listen to the personal pain of individuals; it's essential to respond to everyone with compassion and kindness; it's wise to recognise that these issues are often complicated. But what happens when minorities disagree?

Christians recognise, from Romans 1, that our thinking as humans is fallen, and so we're never going to be able to define rightly who we are. In the 21st century, we still exchange the truth about God for a lie. At the moment the unspoken beliefs run a bit like this:

- *There is no God…* so we worship ourselves.

- *There is no eternity…* so we must have what we desire now.

- *There is no truth…* so I can be whatever I say that I am.

Yet self-worship rapidly leaves us empty. Nothing we create can spark satisfying praise in us like the one and only living God. In the midst of cultural confusion, we can, with relief, turn back to the clarity that God gives us in the Bible and confidently declare these truths:

- *There is a God…* and in looking outside of ourselves to worship him there is wonderful joy. It's the difference between finding wonder in a Lego brick or the Eiffel Tower.

- *There is an eternity…* so we can put aside what we think will provide instant gratification for what will certainly bring more substantial joy.

- *God tells us the truth…* so we can know what it means to enjoy an identity that is given rather than suffer the confusion of trying to create one.

In Romans 1 the apostle Paul says that our thinking is confused, but in the rest of the letter he goes on to unfold the true gospel with wonderful clarity. Here is secure ground for confidence and resilience. Here is the genuine antidote to low self-esteem. Here is hope when we feel like misfits in our own bodies or like strangers among our friends. Here is truth which allows us to admit our weaknesses and struggles, and yet to know that we are of unimaginable value to God our Father:

All have sinned and fall short of the glory of God, and all are justified freely by his grace through the redemption that came by Christ Jesus. (Romans 3 v 23-24)

God demonstrates his own love for us in this: while we were still sinners, Christ died for us. (5 v 8)

There is now no condemnation for those who are in Christ Jesus. (8 v 1)

I am convinced that neither death nor life, neither angels nor demons, neither the present nor the future, nor any powers, neither height nor depth, nor anything else in all creation, will be able to separate us from the love of God that is in Christ Jesus our Lord. (8 v 38-39)

6. GENDER AND SEXUALITY: HOW SHOULD I DEFINE MYSELF?

"If you marry the spirit of your generation, you will be a widow in the next."
William Inge, Playwright

Chelsea Attonley was born as a boy and given the name Matthew. He started dressing as a girl from the age of three. Aged 18 he took the name Chelsea, and paid to have large breast implants and a further implant to shrink his penis and testicles. He planned to have full gender-reassignment surgery at a later date.

However, by age 30, Chelsea had decided to live as Matthew again. This required testosterone injections to restore the body to that of a male again. Chelsea lived as Matthew for two years. During this time, he gave a TV interview in which he observed, "The surgery on the outside does make you feel a lot better, but inside you're the same person. Nothing has altered inside."

Despite the reverse transition, the loss of a womanly body eventually caused Matthew to become depressed, and in 2015, after an attempted suicide, he decided to live as a woman again. Chelsea's life tragically ended in August 2016. The body was found on Chelsea's birthday.

One week before that, someone on Chelsea's Facebook page had asked, "Are you happy as you are now?" Chelsea replied, "I hope one day, and I am learning... I'm not at self-love yet."[5]

Matthew/Chelsea's story is a devastating and deeply moving example of the search for identity. It's tragic that he never heard of (or at least never understood) God's love—a love that takes us as we are but restores us to the image of Jesus, which we're intended to bear. It's a love that really can alter you on the inside. It's a love that provides the honest truth and also the divine affirmation that we all need. Stories like this remind us of how important it is to approach people with compassion.

Yet at the same time, we must be careful not to determine our theology (or public policy) by emotional stories. I suspect most of us do probably allow that to happen sometimes. It may be that we watch a compelling TV documentary of someone in pain and distress because of confusion over their identity. We hear them say that following a particular course of action will make them happy, and we're naturally sympathetic.

It may be that we are affected by a loved one. What do you do when someone you care for greatly says, "I can't help it. I have no choice"? If someone has no choice, it seems deeply unfair to penalise them. Indeed, it might be you who feels that you have no choice over who you are.

The consequence is that we might well be swayed in our views because of a compelling story. That's where many of us find ourselves emotionally.

Having thought a little about the general cultural movement towards self-love and self-creation, we're going to slow down and consider the two most incendiary areas where this plays out today: gender and sexual identities.

These are two topics which most politicians and journalists, and indeed Christians, are nervous about raising because of anxiety about offending the prevailing cultural orthodoxy. I am not attempting a thorough look at either issue. Nor am I challenging the reality of how someone who experiences same-sex attraction or gender dysphoria feels. Instead we're going to try and place both issues within the wider context of who God has made us to be. Wherever we find ourselves on these issues, we need to seek to trust God and let him shape our thinking and emotional responses.

1. "I'm Trapped in the Wrong Body"

Christians tend to lean in one of two directions in discussions around transgender. Some suggest that Jesus would have stood with and protected those experiencing gender dysphoria, while others insist that Jesus would have stood up for truth and denounced any attempt at changing sex.

This is probably because there are broadly two ways in which transgender issues get discussed: as a medical condition and as a radical ideology. The first does indeed demand enormous sympathy and compassion. The latter is deeply damaging. Let me explain.

Gender dysphoria is a recognised medical condition defined as a "marked incongruence between one's experienced gender and assigned gender of at least six months' duration".[6] It seems evident that those suffering with gender dysphoria need help and support, much as those with, say, depression do.

Yet, in more recent years, transgender activists have turned this condition into a radical ideology around the whole area of gender. By "radical ideology" I mean a novel view that is asserted as undeniably true, and which everyone else is expected to accept without question. In this case the view is that gender is largely culturally constructed, that one's gender is not inherently linked to one's body, and that no binary division exists between male and female.

A young woman at our church, who is studying for a psychology degree, reports that a few weeks ago, a lecturer began his lecture by saying, "Hands up if you're male", followed by, "Hands up if you're female." He then declared, "You're all wrong! There is no gender." This was presented as a fact on which no discussion would be tolerated.

This is an ideology that has emerged in more popular culture with the 71 gender options available on Facebook or over 100 on Tumblr. Many local primary schools now engage in the UK's Diversity Week in April of each year. Lots about that is good.

Yet on the issue of gender, some of the organisations involved in shaping this conversation are quite strident. For instance, the LGBT+ anti-violence charity Galop teaches, "Transphobia is intolerance of gender diversity. It is based around the idea that there are only two sexes— male or female, which you stay in from birth".[7]

That's the "idea" which the Bible says is truth. No matter how graciously you hold and present that view, if you trust the Bible on this, Galop define you as "transphobic".

Life in a Fallen World Is Messy

As a consequence of humanity's rebellion recorded in Genesis 3, every human is fallen, and every member of humanity is physically, mentally and sexually broken. For each of us, our bodies, minds and desires malfunction to one degree or another—from dodgy knees to depression, to both lust and lack of desire. In a fallen world, where all of us, in different ways, have a broken identity, we should not be surprised that some struggle with gender dysphoria.

While gender dysphoria is not a phrase we'll find in the Bible, the closest we come to it is in Matthew 19, where

Jesus speaks about eunuchs—men without functioning sexual organs:

¹¹ Jesus replied, "Not everyone can accept this word [not to divorce], but only those to whom it has been given. ¹² For there are eunuchs who were born that way, and there are eunuchs who have been made eunuchs by others—and there are those who choose to live like eunuchs for the sake of the kingdom of heaven. The one who can accept this should accept it." (Matthew 19 v 11-12)

Some are "born as eunuchs". Clearly Jesus recognised that some people are born without appropriate sexual organs— probably what we would now describe as "intersex". While this is not a transgender condition, it too is a product of living in a fallen world, where our minds and bodies fail and where life can be painful and messy.

Others "have been made eunuchs by others"—their condition is unchosen. I was struck by the story that psychologist and author Mark Yarhouse tells about a girl called Ella who was taken to see him for counselling. Ella felt that she was a boy, and three Christian pastors had told her that in this she was sinning. It was an enormous relief to her when Yarhouse told her, "I don't think that you chose to experience your gender incongruence" (*Understanding Gender Dysphoria*, p 58).

Of course, Ella did then face a choice over what she would do. Her experience of incongruence was not chosen, and her feelings were not sinful. But she had to choose whether she would allow her feelings to define her.

Would she say, *I am a girl, but I feel like a boy. Please help me as I try to conform my emotions to the body God has given me.*

Or would she say, *I AM a boy, and I must conform my body to my feelings.*

Currently the loudest voices in society are insisting on the latter. Ella needs enormous compassion and support, but she does not need to allow her feelings to define who she is.

My Body, My Suitcase

"But why not?" one might ask. In a fallen world, isn't it possible that a person's body might be wrong and their feelings right?

The answer to that question rests on how we view our bodies. I recently heard someone suggest that the body is simply a suitcase for the person you are inside. But the Bible indicates that that's not right. The body is not a suitcase or a mere garment that clothes the "real" you. Your body in general, and your body's sex in particular, is highlighted in the Bible as being enormously important and a fundamental part of who you are.

In Genesis 1, humans are introduced into the narrative very differently from every other creature:

21 So God created the great creatures of the sea and every living thing with which the water teems and that moves *about in it, **according to their kinds**, and every winged bird according to its kind. ...*

*24 And God said, "Let the land produce living creatures according to their kinds: the livestock, the creatures that move along the ground, and the wild animals, each **according to its kind." ...***

26 Then God said, "Let us make mankind in our image, in our likeness ... 27 So God created mankind in his own image, in the image of God he created them; male and female he created them. (Genesis 1 v 21, 24, 26-27, emphasis added)

All other creatures are made "according to their kinds"; that is, there are different species within the categories of fish, birds, reptiles and mammals. Yet the only distinction in humanity is male and female. This is so important to notice! The only distinction within the category of humanity is gender. This belongs to the essence of humanity in a way that race, ethnicity or social class do not. All of those differences are secondary. Gender is introduced as essential.

Your sexed body is crucial to who you are. It determines whether you are a father or mother; a daughter or son; a sister or brother. It defines lots of relationships for you.

This means that gender is indeed binary—male and female—and not a spectrum. Our gender is something we are born with; it is not, as has become popular to say, something that we are "assigned" at birth. It is not a social construct. It is objective, not subjective.

The Danger of Self-creation

Janice Turner, a journalist for the British newspaper *The Times*, wrote recently of how, for the first time in her life, she had written to the BBC to complain about a Radio 4 programme.

The programme had interviewed a ten-year-old called Leo along with Leo's mother. Leo had been born as a girl, but her mother had decided that her daughter was not truly a girl when, aged three, "Leo" had insisted that she wanted a pirate party and not a princess one. The mum had decided that this must mean that her daughter was a trans boy. She told "Leo" this, and so, from the age of three, she referred to the child as "he", dressed "him" in male clothes and changed the child's name.

At the age of eight, "Leo" said that "he" wanted to wear girl's clothes and would like to play with Barbie dolls. The mother carried out further internet research and consequently decided that her child was "between genders". At the time of the interview, Leo identified as "gender non-binary".

I don't suppose that this is very common. However, here is the reason for Janice Turner's complaint: she observed that the interviewer "did not once challenge this mother" as to whether it was appropriate to ask a three-year-old, "Darling, are you a boy or a girl?"[8]

Here is one journalist asking what many would feel is an obvious question, and highlighting that an overly rigid

93

view of which toys are appropriate for girls or boys is absurd. However, the interview was carried out as if the mother had acted in an entirely appropriate fashion.

While I don't have any daughters, of my four goddaughters I observe that some have always been pink-princess-loving kids, and others have been rugby-playing pirate-lovers. I'm very glad their parents didn't have such a rigid framework which insisted that to be pirate-loving = trans boy.

Some medics are now giving similar warnings about the dangers of leaping to hasty conclusions. In 2016 the American College of Paediatricians spoke up against the practice of providing puberty-suspending drugs for kids who believe they're of the opposite gender: "Young children are being permanently sterilised and surgically maimed under the guise of treating a condition that would otherwise resolve in over 80% of them. This is criminal."[9] (This was not a popular conclusion, but it was maintained and the paper was updated in September 2017 in response to criticism.)

In other words, we should not let young children define themselves by their feelings. These feelings may well change—80% of the time, such children grow up to be adults who do not want to change sex.

If a young person begins to say that they feel that they're in the wrong body, then they need great compassion and gentleness in response. However, we also should recognise that childhood and adolescence can be confusing times when most young people are exploring their identity.

The natural question to ask is this: what will make this person happy? It's worth taking a longer view of the answer. The modern solution is to encourage a child to change their gender expression—but will we still think that's a good idea in 50 years' time? The timeless truth is that real happiness is found in embracing the identity God has given us, even when that is hard. Like Ella in the example above, each of us needs to conform our emotions to the body God has given us, with the compassion and support of others around us.

Chelsea Attonley spent her life pursuing self-love as the route to happiness, but she never found it. It's God love that she needed, and it's the same love that we need too.

2. "I Was Born Gay"

Another area where our culture tells us to follow our feelings is in the area of sexual identity. We've covered enough of Genesis 1 – 2 already to establish that God's intended setting for sexual relationships is in the relationship between a man and a woman as husband and wife: "A man leaves his father and mother and is united to his wife, and they become one flesh" (Genesis 2 v 24). (But if you're not convinced, we'll come back to this in the next chapter.)

For years the growing acceptance and celebration of homosexuality has been linked to the assumption that people are born this way. It's the idea that we must not deny people the right to live this way when they have no choice; it's who they are.

This seems so obvious to us. However, there are also a number of secular and practising gay commentators challenging the idea that we have absolutely no choice when it comes to sexual orientation.

The newspaper columnist and former politician Matthew Parris is well known as an openly gay man. Yet he has observed:

"Same-sex male attraction used to be something you do, not something you are. We are not two separate tribes: the straight and the gay." (The Times, 21 Apr 12)

His argument is that "sexual orientation is less fixed than we suppose". Indeed, he thinks that people can change from pursuing homosexual practice to heterosexual practice and vice versa. He is cautious in his language and aware that some will view him as "betraying the cause", but he is very uncomfortable with the modern insistence that someone is born gay or straight and that these are either/or positions that do not change. He hates the plea, "I can't help it".

Parris is reacting against a sleight of hand which says, "You're a man who finds some men attractive? Then you ARE gay—even if you never act upon it. Your feelings reveal the very essence of who you are."

His position is more along these lines: *So, you're a man who finds some men attractive? Then you now have a choice to make. You could pursue a same-sex relationship; you could lead a celibate life; or, if you are sexually attracted to both sexes, you could choose a heterosexual relationship.*

This is actually reasonably close to the Bible's position. Scripture is upfront about the fact that in a fallen world all of us will have some feelings and emotions which are fallen and sinful. But these do not define us. If you feel attracted to people of the same sex, that need not define you. It does not "make you gay". You choose whether to engage in same-sex intercourse or not, and you choose whether to build your identity around such relationships or not.

Similarly, in 2015, the noted lesbian scholar Lisa Diamond published an article in *The New Scientist* entitled "Sexuality is fluid—it's time to get past "born this way". She writes:

"It is time to just take the whole idea of sexuality as immutable, the 'born this way' notion, and just come to a consensus as scientists and as legal scholars that we need to put it to rest. It's unscientific, it's unnecessary, and it's unjust." (The New Scientist, 22 Jul 15 and follow up interview 25 Jul 15)

She can point to lots of research supporting her point, especially studies involving identical twins where one is same-sex attracted and the other is not. Sexual orientation is not purely a predetermined feature fixed before birth. A recent piece of Canadian research combined the results of

2,300 clinical studies on whether we are primarily shaped by nature or nurture. The overall picture suggested that we are 52% the product of our genes and 48% the product of our environment. Our views and emotions are a combination of both nature and nurture; both innate predispositions and environmental factors play a part. And when it comes to sexuality, a new piece of research in 2019 showed that genetic factors accounted for about 32% of whether someone will have same-sex sex.[10]

Yet for several decades the idea that some people are "born gay" has dominated the headlines in our society, and so most people assume it's true. It's therefore unsurprising that people lean towards believing that it's unfair if people "born gay" can't marry.

Whatever it is that causes our attractions to tend one way or another, each of us has a choice on how we respond to our feelings. As Paul reminds the Corinthian church:

[9] *Do not be deceived: neither the sexually immoral nor idolaters nor adulterers nor men who have sex with men* [10] *nor thieves nor the greedy nor drunkards nor slanderers nor swindlers will inherit the kingdom of God.* [11] *And that is what some of you were. But you were washed, you were sanctified, you were justified in the name of the Lord Jesus Christ and by the Spirit of our God. (1 Corinthians 6 v 9-11)*

He tells these Christians not to be deceived. Just because certain patterns of behaviour have been normalised in society, it doesn't mean they're acceptable to God. Don't be deceived by their offer of fulfilment. Giving into your feelings—allowing yourself to be defined by them—might promise emotional fulfilment, but it cannot deliver. But Jesus offers something far better: "Whoever is united with the Lord is one with him in spirit" (v 17). When you become a Christian, you are washed clean and given the strength to choose to live for Jesus.

Making Choices

The main point of this book is that identity is not something we choose or create for ourselves—it is God-given. Even if we are conflicted about our gender or sexuality, there remains a choice about whether to listen to God or to follow our feelings. Yet the loudest voices in society are screaming that there is no choice. They argue that some are born gay and others are born in the wrong body, and we therefore have a moral obligation to defend and promote the freedom of such people to live in line with these "realities".

Whether you're a confused cultural onlooker or you're emotionally involved as a friend or relative, you should resist the cultural pressure that says people are defined by their feelings. Some medics and secular commentators are now contradicting this. More importantly, the Bible does not define humans by their sexuality or the gender that someone feels themselves to be. It defines us objectively, and part of that is as men or women. The Lord knows that we live in a fallen world where many will wrestle with issues of gender and sexuality, but the Bible encourages us to honour him. And it encourages every one of us fallen sinners to look forward to the day when all God's people will be perfected in the new creation—when all issues of identity and sexuality will be healed.

If you're reading this as a Christian who is struggling with feelings and emotions that make you desire to act in a way which would not honour the God who loves you, you need to know that your feelings *do not* define who you are. This is not to deny that you feel a certain way, but it is to insist that you have a choice in how you react to those feelings.

God has defined you as made in his image. You don't have to grope around to construct an identity for yourself. You are not at the mercy of how you feel. And know this: the Lord Jesus sympathises with you as you wrestle with temptation. Jesus was a man who shouted out to God with loud cries and tears, who knew a temptation beyond any that we will face—but who was true to himself by remaining true to the mission the Father had given him.

7. SEX: THE HUNGER OF SELF-GRATIFICATION?

"Imaginary evil is romantic and varied; real evil is gloomy, monotonous, barren, boring. Imaginary good is boring; real good is always new, marvellous, intoxicating."
Simone Weil, Gravity and Grace

You've reached that chapter on sex. Not that you may have guessed that from the quote above. But it's an insightful line, and I chose it because you could equally replace a few words to make it read:

"Imaginary casual sex is romantic and varied; real casual sex is gloomy, monotonous, barren, boring. Imaginary faithfulness is boring; real faithfulness is always new, marvellous, intoxicating."

One of the most common expressions of the contemporary need to be "true to self" is sexual activity: it is believed that the more freedom we have to pursue the sex that we desire without shame, the happier we'll be. With sex, as with all areas of life, the following philosophy applies: *if it feels good and no one seems to be getting hurt, do it.*

People increasingly assume that to break all traditional sexual boundaries (many of which overlap with biblical boundaries) is "romantic and varied". The truth is that it leaves you bored and emotionally hungry.

By contrast, the Bible's vision of a sexual relationship—as a life-long, monogamous, self-giving commitment—is often mocked as dull or restrictive. Nothing could be further from the truth. As we saw in chapter 3, God has designed us for intimate, interdependent relationships, which means that self-giving commitment to another person turns out to be more satisfying than living for yourself. With sex, as with all areas of life, if we really want to know the freedom of being true to ourselves, we need to be true to our status as God's image-bearers and conduct our relationships in the way that God says we're designed for.

My Right or My Hobby?

Modern culture is rather divided about how to view sex. On the one hand, some have a distorted but exalted view of sex as *the* source of relational intimacy. By this logic, to deny oneself (or other people) an intimate romantic relationship is repressive—which is not just unhealthy but dangerous—because it withholds something so important for relational and emotional health.

This is the reasoning which has led some within the church to embrace gay marriage: how can someone be happy if they are denied a loving sexual relationship? More often this assumption is unspoken: if relationships cannot be intimate without sex, then if I'm not having consensual sex, I'm missing out on intimacy.

Some would go so far as to say that sex is a fundamental human right. Indeed, the International Women's Health Coalition argues that "sexual rights underpin the enjoyment of all other human rights".[11] This logic has reached a bizarre conclusion with the development of the Incel (involuntary celibate) movement. This is an online subculture of men who adopt the language of civil rights and claim that they have a right to sex because it is a fundamental human need—much as others claim a basic right to be housed, fed and have some level of healthcare provided by the state.

While some in our society overvalue sex as absolutely essential, it is perhaps more common to undervalue sex by viewing it as merely a physical activity. It's just an appetite like hunger or an activity like playing tennis. Therefore, like tennis, it's worth trying to improve your technique with practice, and it's more fun to play with multiple partners. Naturally, it follows that there should never be any guilt or regret attached to sexual activity—you just need to move on.

What a contrast with the Bible's high view of sex as being the means by which a husband and wife become "one flesh". It's a physical expression of the new "unit" that two people become when they marry, and it's a holy, God-given "glue" to aid emotional intimacy within that marriage.

Yet there is little new in the view that sex merely satisfies an appetite. Here's Paul responding to such claims in 1 Corinthians 6:

> [12] "I have the right to do anything," you say—but not everything is beneficial. "I have the right to do anything"—but I will not be mastered by anything. [13] You say, "Food for the stomach and the stomach for food, and God will destroy them both." The body, however, is not meant for sexual immorality but for the Lord, and the Lord for the body. [14] By his power God raised the Lord from the dead, and he will raise us also. [15] Do you not know that your bodies are members of Christ himself? Shall I then take the members of Christ and unite them with a prostitute? Never! [16] Do you not know that he who unites himself with a prostitute is one with her in body? For it is said, "The two will become one flesh." [17] But whoever is united with the Lord is one with him in spirit.   (1 Corinthians 6 v 12-17)

When it comes to sex, these Corinthian Christians have been hoodwinked by the claims of their culture. But Paul offers them, and us, a better way to think about sex and relationships.

Claim 1: "We're Free When We Indulge"

In verse 12 Paul quotes some in Corinth who deploy a very modern-sounding slogan: "I have the right to do anything". Or as we might say, *I'm free to do whatever I want. If it's not against the law and it's between consenting adults, what's wrong with some sexual fun?* Paul's response is that not everything is beneficial. Just because something is legal in the eyes of the state and permissible in the eyes of society, it does not mean it's good for you: "Not everything is beneficial".

This is true even on a sociological level, never mind a spiritual one. Take, for example, the area of pornography. Various studies in the UK show that more and more men in their 20s and 30s are seeking help with erectile dysfunction. Medical professionals suggest that this is, in large part, due to young men watching unrealistic portrayals of sexual endeavour in internet porn, and then suffering related "performance anxiety" when it comes to real-life sexual encounters.[12] It turns out that unlimited pornography does not deliver unlimited sexual pleasure and freedom, but rather a generation of young men who are anxious about their "performance". It doesn't sound as if porn has been beneficial.

Similarly the author Allison Pearson wrote recently of her shock at being told by one doctor friend about the increasing number of teenage girls she was treating with internal injuries. These were caused by repeated anal sex when "their bodies are simply not designed for that"—but the girls said it was what boys expected.[13] That doesn't sound beneficial either.

In the second half of verse 12 Paul answers the Corinthians' slogan with a comment about freedom: "I will not be mastered by anything". His point is that what looks like liberty will often leave us enslaved.

The modern world is characterised by insatiable desire, and in most areas of life we're accustomed to near-instant gratification—these days you don't even have to wait *24 hours* to receive your latest Amazon purchase. Internet advertisers work on a principle of seven seconds. They have to grab someone's attention within seven seconds or else the potential customer will click elsewhere and move on.

That desire for quick gratification carries into the area of sexual activity. We want it and feel that we need to have it now—and in the 21st century, we often can "have it now". But this is not true freedom. I was struck years ago in reading a letter that the author C.S. Lewis sent to his friend Keith Masson, in which he speaks of masturbation and the danger of self-gratification (and of course, what he says is true for women too):

"[Masturbation] sends a man back to the prison of himself, there to keep a harem of imaginary brides ... the harem is always accessible, always subservient, calls for no sacrifices or adjustments ... Among those shadowy brides he is always adored, always the perfect lover; no demand is made on his selfishness. In the end they become the medium in which he increasingly adores himself, in a way no woman can rival."

In life, and certainly in the Christian life, the mark of real maturity is to escape the prison of self-absorption. Masturbation can lock you in. Although some marriages do practise masturbation with mutual consent, normally masturbation is the opposite of self-giving love. It is self-gratification. If you always give in to your urges, then you are not free; you're enslaved. This is not freedom.

By contrast, reserving sex (and by that I mean all sexual activity) for inside a marriage brings great benefits and freedoms. In that context there is a commitment to love, even when things go wrong. There is no pressure "to perform" because you're in this together "for better or for worse". And in a marriage, your spouse is not part of an imaginary harem and is not a shadowy bride/groom who will not challenge you. They will tell you when you're being an idiot and help you to grow, within the secure embrace of a promise to love. Of course, most marriages experience difficulty with sex at some point. But where there is commitment and a self-giving attitude, you can work through it. There is wonderful freedom in knowing that a spouse will not reject you.

Claim 2: "Sex Is Only an Appetite"

The second slogan that Paul addresses in verse 13 is an ancient version of "sex is only an appetite". He quotes the Corinthians as saying, "Food for the stomach and the stomach for food". In other words, *I have urges and ways of meeting them. When I'm hungry, I eat food. When I'm randy, I have sex.*

At the turn of the 21st century this slogan hit a new low with the lyrics of the song "The Bad Touch", which was a top-ten hit in multiple countries and, after remixes, for multiple bands:

"You and me baby, ain't nothin' but mammals, so let's do it like they do on the Discovery Channel."

A reminder from chapter 1: we're not just mammals; we're made in God's image. Why would we even want to copy animal behaviour?! They sit in the pouring rain without taking shelter, they eat raw flesh, and their toilet habits are not polite! I don't see many people rushing to copy them there. More acutely, as Stanley Grenz observes, "In most animal species, including most primates, the male must be more dominant than the female before she will allow copulation" (Stanley Grenz, *Sexual Ethics*, p 39). Few people would recommend that we "do it" like that.

We're not just mammals, and so sex does not merely satisfy an appetite, nor is it simply sensory pleasure. Sexual activity in the Bible is always viewed as relational:

Adam made love to [literally, "knew"] his wife Eve, and she became pregnant. (Genesis 4 v 1)

[Sarai] said to Abram, "The LORD has kept me from having children. Go, sleep with [literally, "go into"] my slave; perhaps I can build a family through her." (Genesis 16 v 2)

And Absalom never said a word to Amnon, either good or bad; he hated Amnon because he had disgraced [meaning "raped"] his sister Tamar. (2 Samuel 13 v 22)

Whereas we might say "slept with", "had sex with" and "raped", the Hebrew Old Testament says "he knew her", "went into her" and "disgraced/oppressed her". All of these have much more of a relational tone to them: A does something to B.

In modern language sex has ceased to be automatically relational—we say A and B "had sex". Sex has become an activity: in effect, a third party, almost distinct from the two people involved. As theologian Harvey Cox wrote all the way back in the 1960s:

"Playboy and its less successful imitators are not 'sex magazines' at all. They dilute and dissipate authentic sexuality by reducing it to an accessory, by keeping it at a safe distance."[14]

But the Bible says that sex is not just something we do; it's the means by which two people physically become one flesh in a way which strengthens their bond emotionally.

When we lose this relational sense of sexual intercourse, sex can soon centre on gratification of the self. We may well live in a consumer age—but people are *not* consumables.

But Seriously... What's the Problem?

Still we might say, "If there's consent and no one gets hurt, what's the problem?"

I'd contend that there are two problems.

The first is the impact on you. Some people have casual sex because they think it's about a mere appetite. Others embark on sexual relationships hoping that these will make them feel wanted, and fill that longing which we all have for intimacy. Yet to borrow the haunting phrase of the poet W.B. Yeats, multiple sexual partners can lead to "the perpetual virginity of the soul". That is, the emotional fulfilment you desire always eludes you when you seek it in casual sex. It's almost as if every time you sleep with someone new, you paint a layer of emotional protection over yourself. The more partners you have, the more layers of paint are applied, so that eventually to strip everything away and have a genuine emotional attachment to someone becomes harder.

The second problem is the impact on the other person. Although people say that consent is not hard to understand, it clearly is: for example, first-year students in some universities are now having to have lessons in what consent means. You can now get "consent apps" with which two people record their formal agreement on their phones—just in case things get tricky later. Yet even then, if there's only nominal consent given under emotional pressure, that's still not right.

As an example of the dangers, let me quote, with permission, from an email I received a while back after preaching on 1 Corinthians 6:

"Dear Matt,

"As I listened to the talk on sexual immorality last night, I was reassured that Christ washes us clean of all our sins. However, I was also reminded of the pain sexual sin causes.

"I am struggling with the split from an ex-boyfriend a few years ago. It was a painful one because whilst we were both Christians, he insisted upon us sleeping together before marriage or, he said, that he would have to end it because he needed sex.

"For months I pointed to teaching in the Bible of how this was wrong, and we would spend hours arguing. It would end in tears and the fear that I would lose him. He was my best friend. I wanted us to spend our lives together serving the Lord and couldn't imagine marrying anyone else.

"Sadly, he issued the ultimatum of sleeping together or he would have to end it. That he wouldn't marry someone he hasn't slept with. After five months I gave in, despite knowing it wasn't the correct way of loving him and despite knowing this wasn't the way God wanted either of us to live.

"I felt guilt every time we slept together, and we would argue because, despite everything, I still said I felt this wasn't the correct way God wanted us to live.

"In the end it got too much for me, and I said I really loved him but couldn't sleep with him anymore. He called a 'break', saying he knew I was right deep down. Two weeks later I got a phone call to say he'd met someone else and that he'd already slept with her. I was completely heartbroken."

I can't put in print the word I want to use to describe that guy.

That's a sad story, although I suspect it's not particularly uncommon. But it's a stark illustration of the fact that there is a world of difference between self-giving in a relationship and self-gratification. You might well be able to secure "consent" (despite the other person not really wanting to give it). You might well even be engaged to be married. But in either case, if at that point you have sex, it is not because you love your partner. It is because you want to satisfy yourself. Lust says, "I want gratification, and I want it now (and so do you), regardless of the fact that it would be better for both of us to wait." So, it's a selfish act.

Sex is meant to be an act of mutual submission within marriage to help seal commitment. As in all areas of marriage, sex is meant to be about giving for the other's good, not taking or demanding for your own pleasure. By contrast, lust = sex in the service of "me".

So how should that relationship have played out? I often encourage dating couples to ask two questions when they're in a relationship. If you split up, can you say...

a. that both of you have grown as Christians while you were dating?

b. that you have honoured the other person? (That is, that you have not done anything you regret physically, and have not emotionally suggested you were ready for commitment when you were not.)

If the answer to both of those questions is yes, then it's been a good relationship, even though dating has ended.

If the answer is yes, there need not be awkwardness or guilt between the two of you going forward. If the answer is yes, then the relationship has been a good thing, even though it didn't lead to marriage.

In these kinds of relationships, friendship has been valued more than sex. And that's also a healthy place to be in if the dating relationship *does* end in a wedding, as sex within marriage is a glue for that "friendship" (and is not meant to be more important than it).

Self-gratification leaves messy, awkward relationships in its wake. Self-giving builds people up and helps them to flourish; and it can hold its head high.

You're Worth so Much More!

In case this is all sounding a bit negative, notice that Paul continues in 1 Corinthians 6 by reminding the Christians of an extraordinary truth—their bodies belong to Jesus:

15 Do you not know that your bodies are members of Christ himself? Shall I then take the members of Christ and unite them with a prostitute? Never! 16 Do you not know that he who unites himself with a prostitute is one with her in body? For it is said, "The two will become one flesh." 17 But whoever is united with the Lord is one with him in spirit.

18 Flee from sexual immorality. All other sins a person commits are outside the body, but whoever sins sexually, sins against their own body. 19 Do you not know that your bodies are temples of the Holy Spirit, who is in you, whom you have received from God? You are not your own; [20] you were bought at a price. Therefore honour God with your bodies.   *(1 Corinthians 6 v 15-20)*

There *is* something different about sexual sin, according to Paul in verse 18. Sex is an act of intimacy that involves the whole person. It's not that sexual sin is worse in God's sight than other sins, but it can scar us more deeply and make subsequent emotional attachment harder. So Paul's command is "Flee". Not amble. Not dither. Flee.

And flee with the secure knowledge that you are loved. Paul tells believers that they are each a temple of the Holy Spirit (v 19). The picture is meant to bring up thoughts of Solomon's temple in the Old Testament. That temple took 13 years to build and used 750 tonnes of gold (worth roughly £36 or $45+ trillion).

Paul says that *you* are a temple. You are not just a mammal. You are worth far more to the Lord than that physical place in Jerusalem. You were planned for much longer than thirteen years; the Lord planned to save you before the creation of the world. And you cost more than £36 trillion; you were bought at an extraordinary price—the death of Jesus Christ.

In the heat of the moment, when you wonder if you will flee, you need to know that you have a Father who planned to save you, a Saviour who died to redeem you, and a Spirit who lives within you.

And this means that whatever you've done in your past and however reading this chapter has made you feel, God's grace is on offer.

Sharing the Lord's Supper at my church is always a powerful reminder of that. There have been occasions when I've looked around and thought, "How glorious forgiveness is! I'm sharing the cup with people who (either before becoming Christians or subsequently) have had adulterous affairs, have visited prostitutes, have worked as prostitutes, have been addicted to pornography, have had premarital sex or have viewed abusive pornography, as well as those who in their self-righteousness think that they are better than others in the room."

Yet all of us approach the Lord's throne of grace in the same way—through the blood of Jesus Christ shed for our sins. And that means all of us are in communion with him—we are "united with the Lord [and are] one with him in spirit" (v 17).

"Therefore," says Paul, "honour God with your bodies" (v 20). If you're a Christian, you know that Jesus sacrificed himself for you, and he calls you to follow him on the path of self-giving in relationships, not self-gratification. It brings him honour, and it *will* leave you happier.

But Aren't I Missing Out?

That picture of believers united around the Lord's Supper is also what you need to be reminded of if you've read this chapter with the sad suspicion that because you're not married, you're missing out on something.

Last year we carried out a survey among a few churches in which one of the questions was "Do you think your desire for relationship will be best met in marriage or friendship?" I wasn't that surprised that across several hundred people in the 18-35 age bracket, 63% answered "marriage". 31% were "not sure", but only 6% replied "friendship".

Often in churches, marriage is exalted as the only real way of finding intimate relationship. I doubt that too many churches would ever say, "Without marriage you'll end up lonely", but I guess that can feel like their implicit message. That's deeply unhelpful. For some, close friendship will be found in marriage. For others it is not and never will be. But while sex fosters intimacy within marriage, you need neither sex nor marriage to experience real intimacy. We'll return to this theme in chapter 9, but remember that "single and celibate" is *not* second best.

A little while ago I was speaking on this topic for another church. Afterwards I spoke to an individual who had been sleeping with someone of the same sex. During the relationship they had wondered about giving up on Jesus altogether. It had clearly been an emotionally tumultuous few months, but eventually they had broken off the relationship and started coming to church regularly again. Their comment was, "Honestly, I was weighing up which way I was going to jump. When it came to it, I couldn't bring myself to reject the promises of Scripture. But emotionally, it was the friendships that I had with people at church that kept me. I realised that they cared for me and meant more to me than my lover did."

That's a healthy church—where someone who has chosen to live a celibate life can testify that they have found deep, committed, nurturing relationships. It's the kind of church culture that needs the whole church family to commit to self-giving rather than self-gratification in every kind of relationship.

Sexual liberation promises much, but self-gratification delivers little. True freedom and true fulfilment can only be found when we give of ourselves. We'll consider that next.

8. RELATIONSHIPS: DENY YOURSELF TO FIND YOURSELF

"There is only one thing which is generally safe from plagiarism—self-denial."

G.K. Chesterton

A few years ago, a young couple at our church happily announced a pregnancy. But at their 20-week scan, they were told that the baby had serious congenital deformities. The doctor said it was very unlikely that the baby would make it to term, and that even if she did, she would die outside of the womb in a few hours or days at most. They were told in no uncertain terms to abort.

The couple said no.

As Christians, they believed it was wrong to terminate their baby's life. Their doctor was incredulous, asking why on earth they would cause themselves such distress and pain. Many of their friends thought they were mad to put themselves through such emotional upheaval and told them to take the easy way out.

After they had determined to continue the pregnancy as long as possible, I remember sitting at our dining table and praying with them. In the face of numerous medics and friends telling them to stop and save themselves needless pain, continuing the pregnancy felt like a costly thing to do. The couple insisted that some things were more important than making life easy.

This is what self-denial looks like. This couple were resolved not to do what was easiest or most comfortable, but what was right. The next few months were indeed hard and emotionally painful, particularly in the final few months of pregnancy when the mother carried a child that she expected would die very quickly. There were inevitable moments when they asked, "Why are we doing this to ourselves?"

Yet their baby girl was born safely, albeit very small and with a few complications, and is now a much-loved and thriving member of their family. Afterwards, some friends were brave enough to admit that their advice was wrong. They were pleased that the couple had for several months denied their own comfort and endured emotional turmoil for the sake of their unborn child. Sometimes we recognise that denying yourself for the sake of another is the right thing to do.

Personal Growth = Good

It's a strange fact that while many will tell their friends to "be true to themselves" and do what's right for them, we still find it undeniably attractive when people deny themselves and put others first.

In movies, we love the narrative arc in which the hero overcomes some moral flaw and gives of themselves for the good of others. In the film *Groundhog Day*, Bill Murray's character has to repeat the same day over and over until he finally stops being selfish and is impelled to become kind and generous. We think, "I'm glad you've not been allowed to listen to your own feelings indefinitely, but have had them confronted and have changed". Part of the joy in the original *Star Wars* film is that when the Rebels are at the point of failure, selfish, cynical Han Solo, who has only lived for himself, returns to save the day. Phew! We're so glad he didn't listen to his selfish feelings!

While most people in modern society have rejected the language of sin, we still speak of personality flaws and think it's good to conquer them. People aspire to grow, change and learn. Deep down, although our culture espouses the line "be true to yourself", there is also an awareness that denying yourself may well be a good thing to do as well, if it leads to maturity of character and is better for others. This is an unsurprising truth for anyone who has read the Bible!

To Be a Christian = to Deny Yourself

Jesus is very blunt about the cost of following him. I was reading the Bible one-to-one with a guy who had recently become a Christian. When we came to Mark 8, he commented, "Jesus demands absolutely everything from us, and doesn't even say sorry or apologise. He's clearly not an Englishman."

Well, yes, that's one way of putting it...

34 Then he called the crowd to him along with his disciples and said: "Whoever wants to be my disciple must deny themselves and take up their cross and follow me. 35 For whoever wants to save their life will lose it, but whoever loses their life for me and for the gospel will save it. 36 What good is it for someone to gain the whole world, yet forfeit their soul? 37 Or what can anyone give in exchange for their soul? 38 If anyone is ashamed of me and my words in this adulterous and sinful generation, the Son of Man will be ashamed of them when he comes in his Father's glory with the holy angels." (Mark 8 v 34-38)

There is no ambiguity here. In verse 34 Jesus demands three things. The first is that we deny ourselves. That's not denying yourself a few little treats, like giving up chocolate for Lent or alcohol in January—that's *relatively* easy. No, Jesus is asking us to give up control for life. That means no longer asking, "What would I like to do?" but rather, "What does Jesus want me to do?"

Second, Jesus tells us to "take up [our] cross". That ratchets up the demand. It adds the idea of denying yourself in public with a possible cost of humiliation: a willingness to suffer for public allegiance to Christ.

Third, Jesus tells us to "follow him". Without this last command, the first two would be overwhelming and crippling. Jesus says we're to follow *him*, and that means that we'll have with us the personal presence of Jesus by his Spirit as we seek to deny ourselves. His presence can turn discipleship from drudgery into joy. We don't follow a principle but a person—the man who is God.

Of course, Jesus does give us a further incentive. He tells us in four overlapping phrases that "whoever wants to save their life will lose it, but whoever loses their life for me and for the gospel will save it" (v 35).

I find myself occasionally shouting a warning at my teenage son and his friends as they cross a road while playing a game on their phones. You're an idiot if you stay alive in a computer game but get run over in real life. Jesus makes the bigger point that you're a fool if you save your life now—holding on to your freedom by living for yourself—but lose your life in eternity. Jesus says, *I died to save your eternal life, so follow me. Don't throw eternity away. Follow me.*

We deny ourselves because it's the right thing to do—because it's what Jesus calls us to. But more than that, following Jesus looks beautiful when we consider how it impacts others.

Consider Others More

Take the hymn that Paul quotes in Philippians 2:

³ *Do nothing out of selfish ambition or vain conceit. Rather, in humility value others above yourselves,* ⁴ *not looking to your own interests but each of you to the interests of the others.*
⁵ *In your relationships with one another, have the same mindset as Christ Jesus:*
⁶ *who, being in very nature God,*

> *did not consider equality with God something to be*
> *used to his own advantage;*

⁷ *rather, he made himself nothing*

> *by taking the very nature of a servant,*
> *being made in human likeness.*

⁸ *And being found in appearance as a man,*

> *he humbled himself*
> *by becoming obedient to death—*
> > *even death on a cross!*

Wow, that's countercultural: value the interests of other people more than your own.

We're told to have the same mindset as Jesus—which was, essentially, one of *I'm putting others first.* It would have been entirely reasonable for the Son of God to declare, *I'm equal with God the Father, so I'm not going put myself out for humans—why doesn't he take the nature of a servant?*

Wonderfully, Jesus did not say that.

He could have said, *Humanity is a bunch of ungrateful parasites—living off my creation, not paying me their due respect. Why serve them?*

Wonderfully, Jesus did not say that.

Instead, the one who was "in very nature God" took "the very nature of a servant" (v 6, 7). That's the posture that he chose. Imagine if Queen Elizabeth II knocked on my front door and offered to wash my car down. That would be weird... inappropriate... and surprising. Yet it would be as nothing compared to God the Son taking the nature of a servant and living among us.

And having done that, he didn't then say, *Well, I've come to earth to serve humanity, but now I'm here, they remain ungrateful. I've taught them, fed them and healed them, and they still don't get it. Right, that's it; I draw the line here.* Personally, I'm always tempted to think that way. I may give up time, energy and money to help someone, but if I feel a little unappreciated, I'll retreat and say, "Enough".

Jesus didn't. No, he took another step down by humbling himself even further: "by becoming obedient to death—even death on a cross!" Jesus denied himself to achieve eternal good for you and me. That's what Jesus is like. He's the one who flung stars into space, formed the mountains, created the oceans... and he gave himself for others. Even as Jesus drew his final breath, he was still sustaining the breath of those who were killing him. Even as the crowd mockingly called him king, he was still ruling over creation. He is in very nature God, yet he took the nature of a servant.

The one who made you and me reveals that being true means giving yourself away. Jesus denied himself for the good of others, and that is what Christians are called to do. Paul gives us this extraordinary glimpse inside the mind of Jesus and says, "Have the same mindset" (v 5).

Sometimes we might even recognise that living this way is for our good. In 2016 the British comedy actress Sally Phillips made a documentary about the genetic disorder Down Syndrome. Her eldest of three sons has DS, and so the programme celebrated how valuable and precious life with the condition can be. Observing that 90% of British women terminate their pregnancy if they test positive for DS, she commented, "Back then, if you'd asked me if I could cope with a child with disability, I'm not sure whether I would have said yes. Now I would say that having him in my life has changed me and my family—for the better. And that makes me question whether choice is always the wonderful thing it's cracked up to be."

Sally didn't have the test for DS, so she didn't have a choice. Yet she thinks that having a child with a disability, and being forced to put his interests above her own, has changed her and the other members of the family for the better. No doubt it's hard work. No doubt it is, at times, physically and emotionally exhausting. And yet it is for their good.

In smaller ways, I look around at church and see many heroes who place the interests of others ahead of their own—in committing to serve at an international ministry every Friday night; in visiting an elderly member of the church family; in getting to their small groups to encourage others, even though they have to go back to the office afterwards. It's tiring, but they would also say that it is for their own good. Not in a "Cold baths are good for you; they toughen you up" kind of way, but because their character is being changed. They're acting like and becoming more like Jesus. They're slowly becoming the people they were truly designed to be. They're being true to their *best* self.

We really shouldn't be surprised. In his farewell speech to a group of church leaders in Ephesus, Paul told them:

> *In everything I did, I showed you that by this kind of hard work we must help the weak, remembering the words the Lord Jesus himself said: "It is more blessed to give than to receive."* (Acts 20 v 35)

It's more blessed to give than receive. Sometimes, we'll experience the reward that comes from giving of ourselves and our time immediately. We'll feel the joy of deepening relationships with others and with our heavenly Father. We'll delight to act in a way that is a delight to him. And our efforts will bear fruit as friends become Christians, as ministries grow or as people are reconciled. At other times we won't feel particularly blessed. Denying ourselves will leave us feeling tired or sad. Our efforts will go unnoticed or unappreciated. We'll feel the pain of losing our comfort, or losing our money, or even losing our friends. When this is the case, denying ourselves really is an act of faith; we trust we'll be rewarded in heaven.

To live like this you have to know that you will receive an inheritance one million times more than whatever you give up in this life. That's a conviction which has bolstered the decision of some in our church to give up the securities of life and family in the UK to go as missionaries to unreached people groups. It's a truth that has led others to leave their friends here and plant churches in other parts of the city. It looks like madness. But they're looking forward to a day when Jesus will welcome them into his presence in eternity with a hearty "Well done, good and faithful servant".

Until that day, we strive to be faithful to our master's pattern by denying ourselves as he did.

Self-denial in a Marriage

Putting others first is central to Christian living. Yet sometimes it's in the most familiar of relationships that we struggle to do it. That's why I want to apply this in one direction that Jesus does in Mark chapters 8 – 10. This whole section, following his call to "follow me" in 8 v 34, is about what discipleship looks like—it looks like following a crucified king. He talks about pride, working together and battling sin in general, as well as money and levels of wealth. Yet there's one section that seems a little out of place: a passage on marriage and divorce in Mark 10 v 1-12.

Part of the reason it's there is because marriage is a place of discipleship and self-denial. Not many people think of it that way. In the 19th century, the idea of marrying for love was not paramount. Marriage was mainly for providing food, shelter and security. In the 20th century, while people still desired these basics, marriage was increasingly viewed more as a place of love and companionship. In the 21st century, marriage is typically viewed as a vehicle for self-expression and a platform from which to achieve our goals. So the thinking is (although it may not be expressed as blatantly as this), *I will stay with you and love you IF you make me feel good, IF you help me develop myself, IF I don't find someone else who helps me more.*

One analyst, Professor Finkel of Northwestern University, Illinois, said:

"The best marriages today [in his view, ones which are a platform for self-expression] are better than the best marriages of yesteryear. But the problem is, it's harder ... developing such insight requires a heavy investment of time and psychological resources in the marriage."[15]

Golly, that sounds complicated! Do you need a psychology degree to make a marriage work? It all sounds a little simpler when the Bible says, *Consider your spouse's needs first.*

There are plenty of small (and bigger) disagreements in a marriage which are easily resolved if we consider the other first:

- I want to go out v. I want to stay in.

- I want to see these friends v. ugh they drive me nuts.

- I want to move countries v. but I love it here.

- I want to start a family v. not yet.

- I want a lie in v. but it's your turn to get up with the baby.

Serving a spouse in those daily interactions goes a long way to building a marriage that is a pleasure rather than simply living under the same roof. Being served makes a spouse feel valued, loved and appreciated. When both parties are committed to that kind of serving, then marriage is a very happy place.

But in a culture which says I must be true to myself, if you are not fulfilling me, then I'm obliged to leave you. The question I ask is not "What does my spouse need?" but "Is my spouse meeting my needs?" And if the answer is no, then it can't be immoral to get out of the marriage. Love should feel free and fulfilling. Our modern view of marriage tends to be that it is good while it lasts—a bit like a coat or a pair of shoes. If, over time, it wears out or no longer fits, then it makes sense to part ways and try something new.

In one month I've read multiple articles encouraging me to think that way. The take-homes were...

"The marriage dilemma: is infidelity inevitable?"[16]

"Expecting love, lust and a happy family from marriage is impossible."[17]

"If you're in a bad marriage, don't try to mend it—end it."[18]

But Jesus said something different. When asked by the Pharisees whether it was lawful for a man to divorce his wife, Jesus explained that while the Old Testament law made provision for it, the principle is this: a husband and wife "are no longer two, but one flesh. Therefore what God has joined together, let no one separate" (Mark 10 v 8-9). This sounded so unreasonable to the disciples that they asked Jesus about it later in private.

The disciples had got one thing right: marriage is hard work. But Jesus says it's worth working at. Marriage is a wonderful place of discipleship. Sometimes it's so difficult that you may desire to walk away. But the right thing to do is to deny yourself and keep going.

This is true in families too. Here again, the difference between a belief in self-fulfilment and a willingness to deny self is enormous. People justify walking away from their family by saying stuff like, "If we stay together, the hypocrisy will pollute the children. It's better for them that we're happy." But, in the words of the former High Court judge Paul Coleridge, the reality is that family breakdown produces "a river of human misery".[19] Children of divorced parents are more likely to suffer broken marriages themselves. They are more likely to be unemployed or in low-skilled jobs or in trouble with the police.

These are hard things to read if we've experienced divorce close up, and they are broad generalities. But then, often it is those who *have been* affected by divorce who are most aware of the pain it causes. As one divorced journalist put it:

"It is true, whether we like it or not: children are best brought up by their genetic mum and dad, who are married, not merely cohabiting. They are the ones who have the best outcomes. No matter how inconvenient this fact might be as regards our wish to have sexual intercourse with as many people as humanly possible, it is still nonetheless a fact. And we should not ignore it simply because it cramps our style a little and does not give us the non-judgmental freedom we crave. It is one of the few areas where science agrees with the church."[20]

It may be an "inconvenient" fact when we'd rather be true to our feelings, but remaining committed in marriage will generally produce higher levels of happiness for the family as a whole.

Recently a friend of mine in his mid-40s left his wife and two children for another woman.

He told the kids over dinner, "I deserve this".

To which they replied, "We don't".

Sometimes to be "true to self" means being false to your family.

A Perfect Marriage?

I was struck by reading the obituary of Debo Cavendish, the Duchess of Devonshire, who died a few years ago at the age of 96. She observed that "the perfect marriage is about companionship and friendship, but we don't give it a chance to flourish. The middle part can be very difficult, but in my generation often those who were miserable for a bit ended up as close as can be." By contrast, modern culture holds open a door to anyone finding their marriage hard and says, "Run, escape, be true to yourself. Don't live a life of pretence."

Marriage is indeed a place of discipleship and self-denial, but the rewards are great. In fact, it's impossible to grow a truly wonderful marriage without going through hardship. Overcoming the tough times makes the good times even richer.

If you're reading this and the hardship of marriage seems just too hard, then may I plead with you to get help? Nearly every marriage goes through a phase when at least one spouse wonders if they would be happier leaving. So don't wrestle through this season alone. I cannot keep count of the times when I have spoken to a couple and observed, "You only see two options— this marriage, which is really hard work, or leaving the marriage. But there is a third option: working through the hard things to have a great marriage."

Sometimes that really does take faith: faith that following God's way of sticking at marriage is best; faith that enduring through better and worse, richer and poorer, sickness and health is his desire for you; faith that he rewards commitment and self-denial in eternity; faith that placing self-denial ahead of self-fulfilment will result in a richer relationship.

And God's track record shows that he is more than worthy of that faith. Jesus placed our interests above his own and became a servant to secure our salvation. Yet ultimately he was rewarded and exalted above all others.

> [9] *Therefore God exalted him to the highest place*
> *and gave him the name that is above every name,*
> [10] *that at the name of Jesus every knee should bow,*
> *in heaven and on earth and under the earth,*
> [11] *and every tongue acknowledge that Jesus Christ is Lord,*
> *to the glory of God the Father. (Philippians 2 v 9-11)*

Just as Jesus took two steps "down" in verses 6-8, so here in verses 9-11 the Father lifts him "up" two steps: Jesus is exalted to the highest place, and then he is given the name above every name. Jesus was willing to deny himself to experience the Father's pleasure. He carried a cross in this world but wears a crown in the next. Taking the nature of a servant led to a name above all others.

And he calls us to follow his "down and then up" trajectory. Clearly his self-denial and exaltation were of a different order to ours, but still he says, *Follow me. Look not to your own interests but to the interests of others. It will shape you to be more like me now, and the benefits in eternity are wonderful. In fact, you really cannot lose. Deny yourself to find yourself.* That's the way to rich relationships and great community.

9. COMMUNITY: THERE CAN BE NO LOSERS IN CHURCH

"This Christian life was war—of this I was certain. Who in her right mind ... would go to war without an army?"

Rosaria Champagne Butterfield,
The Secret Thoughts of an Unlikely Convert

Silent discos are a pretty strange experience for spectators. The music is played through personal headphones instead of speakers, so it's really odd when you walk in and find a hundred people wearing headphones, stomping around to music you can't hear. Instead, all you can hear is the clomp, clomp, clomp of people's feet on the floor and then the strange moment where everyone "Woos" together and joins in a line of the chorus. The crowd are clearly having a good time, but if you've just entered the room, then frankly, they look a bit weird! They *are* weird if you can't hear the music.

Those dancers are a little like Christians being watched by a bewildered world. Christians appear joyful, and they clearly have a deep connection to one another—but many unbelievers look on and think we're weird. It's because they can't hear the music of the gospel!

But for Christians, who can hear the gospel, it makes perfect sense to live for Jesus. So, when a watching world says, "You're mad to deny your feelings and not put yourself first", Christians can smile and say, "But if you could hear the music I hear, if you had heard how good Jesus is, you'd understand."

And yet, sometimes, even as part of the party, we find that the music has faded from our headphones. While other people are dancing at full volume, we struggle to catch the beat. We're left shuffling around, feeling a little weird and wondering whether living as a Christian means we're losing out after all. In the last few chapters, we've thought a lot about self-sacrifice and self-denial. But if we're really going to live that way—if we're going to ignore the voices telling us to "trust your feelings", "you do you", "be more selfish", "look after yourself"—then we need to turn up the volume on the music of the gospel.

That's what we're going to do in this chapter. Here's what I want to convince you of: there can be no losers in church.

That's not meant to be an aspirational statement. It's a statement of fact. We know that because Jesus told us so:

> [29] *"Truly I tell you," Jesus replied, "no one who has left home or brothers or sisters or mother or father or children or fields for me and the gospel* [30] *will fail to receive a hundred*

times as much in this present age: homes, brothers, sisters, mothers, children and fields—along with persecutions— and in the age to come eternal life. [31] But many who are first will be last, and the last first." (Mark 10 v 29-31)

When you become a Christian and make sacrifices to follow Jesus, you will not lose out *in this life* nor in the age to come. Imagine an old-fashioned set of scales with two pans suspended from a beam. On one side you put in all you've given up to follow Jesus faithfully, and the pan hits the floor. Then you put into the other side everything you gain *in this life*. That doesn't merely compensate and balance out the scales—they now hit the floor on the gain side. Then perhaps imagine adding to the same side all you gain in eternity: the scales collapse and fall over! When you deny your feelings because you want to be faithful to Jesus, you cannot lose out. You end up massively in credit.

There's a Lot to Give Up

Not that it always looks that way on the surface. Jesus suggests quite a list of things that you may have to give up to follow him: "home or brothers or sisters or mother or father or children or fields [we might say source of income or employment]" (v 29).

We have a few believers in our church from Muslim backgrounds. When they became Christians, they were rejected by their families. One (illegally) lost his job because his employer was a Muslim and made his work unbearable. Another had to flee from her country due to the threat of arrest. They know what Jesus is talking about.

Or I can think of single people who feel the loss of the dream of motherhood or fatherhood acutely. But rather than look for a relationship with a non-Christian, they've given up the prospect of having children to follow Jesus and use their singleness in his service. That's a cost. In an honest moment some have even told me that there's sometimes a little voice running through their heads which says that they're missing out and they need to compensate by putting themselves first.

That said, not all Christians share this expectation that following Jesus involves sacrifice. Matt Moore lived as an actively gay man before he became a Christian in 2010 and resolved to live a celibate life. He observes that back then most Christians congratulated him on his repentance and stood with him. Yet ten years on, increasingly he is told *by other Christians* that his repentance is self-destructive and that it puts others off from becoming believers. He writes of the sort of comments he now receives *from professing Christians*:

"I admire you for the strength you exert every day in suppressing this part of yourself, but you don't have to live like this. God wants you to be happy with a person you find desirable. He will still love you and bless you if you find a man to spend the rest of your life with."[21]

Matt is being told that he is losing out and needlessly so. Jesus tells us that obedience is costly. Yet it is obedience, not disobedience, that leads to blessing. And what a blessing it is...

There's More to Gain

After spelling out the costs of discipleship in verse 29, Jesus then goes on to make his extraordinary promise: whatever you give up, you'll receive more back!

> *"No one ... will fail to receive a hundred times as much in this present age: homes, brothers, sisters, mothers, children and fields—along with persecutions."* (Mark 10 v 29-30)

A hundred times more. Charles Spurgeon told the story of one unusual church member who placed a notice in the weekly church magazine declaring that if anyone had financially lost out due to their following Jesus, he would financially reimburse them. Apparently, the announcement appeared for three months but no one took him up on his offer. Now, that's a little eccentric, but you see the point he was making: when people appreciate how much they've gained, the losses are easy to bear.

Or similarly, if you spill a glass of water on the floor, it causes a mess and is a nuisance. Yet if you pour a glass of water into the sea, you can't even see what you have just poured in. The enormity of the sea absorbs the mess of the glass. In a similar way, when we dwell upon the blessings of the Christian life, the losses can be absorbed in them.

"Well that's ok for you to say," you might be thinking, "but that's definitely not my experience". What do we make of Jesus' words then?

Well, it's important to be clear on what Jesus is and isn't promising. Jesus is not promising a simple life of prosperity, comfort and ease. For one thing, he says that persecutions come along with what is gained. Nor can he mean this promise *literally*, because no one has one hundred mothers. (Which is probably a good thing. I love my mother, but I think a hundred mothers would be suffocating!)

Yet Jesus' point is that if you have lost the relationship with your father because you have become a Christian, then within the church family you will find multiple men who can "father" you: who can offer you the advice you lack and the counsel you need. Likewise, if you lose your house by following Jesus, then the church family will accommodate you. If you lose your income by following Jesus, the church family will support you. If you lose friends by following Jesus, you will gain better friends within the church.

Jesus is talking about the overall package of living as a Christian here and now. Yes, there will be things that you lose, but you will also gain the spiritual benefits of forgiveness, hope, delight and joy. And you'll find in the church family new relationships which have a greater loyalty, honesty and faithfulness than those you've lost: a family with greater insight, commitment and kindness.

The benefits of joining the family of God dwarf the losses of leaving the company of this world.

Remember, Jesus says this not as an aspiration but as a promise. So our churches have the responsibility to ensure that this is true. I can think of multiple members of our church who have, due to following Jesus, suffered a schism in their families, or decided to live as single rather than marry an unbeliever, but who could also say they have received more back.

Yet to be honest, I can also think of others who have *not* known that joy in our church family. We've not loved them well enough; their experience was not of receiving a hundred-fold, and so they have gone elsewhere. It saddens me enormously, but I pray that they have found this promise to be true in another church. Any local church will sometimes fail to fulfil what Jesus promises. Yet the promise remains that within God's wider church this can and should be true for everyone.

When I reflect on these individuals that our church let down, I think it's because we didn't pay the cost of time and effort to ensure that they had the supportive relationships they needed. Many of us reading this need to remember that we are the solution for those who have been forced to leave families and "fields" behind. *We* are the "hundred times as much" that can be gained.

Part of God's provision for those who have paid a heavy relational cost for following Jesus is the way in which he "sets the lonely in families" (Psalm 68 v 6). So if we're already in families—and perhaps we could expand that to well-established friendship groups—God wants us to bring others in.

After all, how can we expect a Muslim convert to accept abandonment by their family if we don't pay the cost of discipleship? How can we expect a convert out of a gay lifestyle to accept celibacy if we don't sacrifice our ease to bring them into our families? If we are not willing to pay these costs of following Jesus, then how can we call others to do so? Instead, we're *all* called to deny ourselves to meet the needs of others.

And in God's gospel economy, when we sacrifice in order to meet another person's "deficits", he pours out a surplus of blessing on us all. For all that it costs, there is great blessing in offering a family to someone who has lost theirs. There is enormous joy in bringing extra "aunts" and "uncles" into the lives of our children. There is real pleasure in being God's instrument to bring relationship to someone who would otherwise be lonely. I can think of individuals at church who have, for example, left the gay community and had a family say, "Come and live with us for as long as you need". Or a woman who left an abusive husband and had a family say, "Come and live with us for as long as you need". Although that placed a level of strain upon these families, there was also enormous pleasure in helping someone at their most vulnerable and lonely to regain emotional stability.

And all this makes for healthier church communities. For some people there may be a lot they have to give up to follow Jesus—but it's far easier if they see the rest of their church family making sacrifices too. So, as we're sharing our lives with one another, it ought to become far more natural to talk about the cost that we are paying, in our own ways. I'm not talking about petty virtue-signalling, but about being honest with a group that knows us well— so that together, we're encouraged to keep giving of ourselves, and keep receiving from Jesus.

The Best Is in Eternity!

So far we've focused on life now, but of course we cannot ignore that the best Christian blessings remain in the future. We'll be with Jesus face to face. We'll be in glory with resurrected bodies. We'll be reunited with people we love. We'll never again know pain or loss. We may have given up houses and fields in this life, but then Jesus will say, *Come and reign over the whole world*. We may have given up a kind of worldly gratification now, but we will enjoy heavenly pleasures in the future.

So when we're struggling to follow Jesus because the cost feels high here, we need to dwell upon where we're going. Heaven is no *mere* compensation for the losses of this life. It is far more abundantly wonderful than anything we can imagine here on earth. We need to remember that—in the words of author C.S. Lewis—this world is merely the "shadowlands", and the world to come is the reality. In this world our bodies are mere acorns compared to the mighty trees that we will become (1 Corinthians 15 v 35-44). The Bible places a huge emphasis on heaven. Our reward is in heaven (Matthew 5 v 12). Our Father is in heaven (Matthew 6 v 9). Our treasure is in heaven (Matthew 6 v 20). Our Master is in heaven (Ephesians 6 v 9). Our Saviour is in heaven (Hebrews 9 v 24). Our brothers and sisters are in heaven (Hebrews 12 v 23). Our inheritance is in heaven (1 Peter 1 v 3-4).

Whatever we give up now, the benefits cannot be added up or counted. They break the scales!

Why There's No Such Thing as "Just a Friend"

One specific way we can make sure that there are "no losers in church" is by valuing our friendships more highly.

Allow me, just for a moment, to climb onto a personal soapbox. For the past few years at my church, I've been on a quest to ban the use of the phrase "They're just a friend".

It comes up, of course, when someone asks, "Is there anything going on between you and X? Are you two dating?" The response can be "No, they're just a friend".

That short sentence instantly condemns friendship as less important than romantic relationships. And that's not true. In our earlier years, boyfriends and girlfriends may come and go, while friends are often constant. Even if we marry, good friendships of many years standing cannot be replaced (even if the dynamic may need to change).

Couples are foolish if they allow good friendships to wither. It's very easy to be lonely inside a marriage.

A far better response to the question "Are you dating them?" would be "No, but it's a friendship I cherish. I don't want romance from it, but I do hope our friendship continues to grow."

If we're going to live as God intended rather than being pulled along by a culture that screams at us to "be true to ourselves", we're going to need Christian friends. And if we're going to ask single Christians to maintain sexual purity, or ask same-sex-attracted Christians to remain celibate, or ask Christians with gender dysphoria to live out the sex that God has given them—then we need to be good friends.

Beside which, friends are one of life's great riches. You may have no money, you might lack power in the world, you may never achieve very much with your life... but if you have good friendships, then you are rich. Again, in the words of C.S. Lewis in *The Four Loves*: "[Friendship] has no survival value; rather it is one of those things which gives value to survival".

Five Ways to Pursue Friendship

Work has deadlines, families can make great demands; and that often means that friendship sinks to the bottom of the to-do list. So let me be really practical in suggesting five things that we can do to develop our own personal friendships and, in doing so, contribute to a wider church culture where people are properly loved and cared for.

1. Invest Time

As I was thinking about the subject, I asked a longstanding friend what had kept our friendship going when, actually, we are not very similar. He's more insightful than me so he immediately came back: "Our friendship is intentional and spiritual". I think he's right.

We have been intentional in making sure we spend time together. When we lived in different countries for five years, we would tend to speak most weeks, or at least fortnightly, on the phone. Now that we live closer together, we still have to be very deliberate about making space in our schedules to see each other. Friendships take time. We're also intentional in the questions we ask and the desire to spur one another on. This means it's impossible to have very close relationships with a dozen people—most of us can only manage 2-4 close friends. Ideally it's good to commit to a handful of friends for life and really seek to be there for them.

2. Have a Spiritual Agenda

I really loved the best man's speech at one wedding I was at recently. After the customary gentle roasting of the groom, he finished by saying, "Thank you for having me as your best man today, but more than that, thank you for making me a better Christian man during the years of our friendship". Isn't that a brilliant testimony!

Great friendships move beyond a common interest. They are built upon the Saviour Jesus, whom we share, and serving him in a common purpose. I've always loved the account of Jonathan and David's friendship. In 1 Samuel 23 David is on the run for his life as King Saul is trying to kill him. He is alone and without friends or supporters. But "Jonathan went to David at Horesh and helped him to find strength in God" (1 Samuel 23 v 16). We're not told the details, but no doubt, Jonathan turned David back to the promises of God and helped strengthen his faith. He did so by going and sitting with him. This little snapshot of their friendship helps explain David's pain years later when he hears of Jonathan's death:

> *I grieve for you, Jonathan, my brother;*
> *you were very dear to me.*
> *Your love for me was wonderful,*
> *more wonderful than that of women.*
>
> *(2 Samuel 1 v 26)*

While there's no doubt that David was flawed as a husband, he was nonetheless clearly one man for whom friendship was a richer blessing than marriage.

3. Let Friendship Groups Be Porous

While we need to be realistic about how many friends we commit to long term, it is also the case that, as people move around and move on, some great friendships may only last a couple of years—and that's ok too. Some people are sent into our lives for us to enjoy for a season. That's partly why I am also keen at church to encourage porous friendship groups. It's hard when you join a church to find yourself on the outside of a clique of people. We can't be close friends with everyone, but we do need to include new people, and especially those who are potentially lonely, in groups and group activities—be it a trip to the cinema or a week's holiday. Our social circles at church should feel inclusive.

4. Bear with One Another's Flaws

Although addressed to the whole church, Colossians 3 also offers realism on how we grow precious friendships:

> [12] *Therefore, as God's chosen people, holy and dearly loved, clothe yourselves with compassion, kindness, humility, gentleness and patience.* [13] *Bear with each other and forgive one another if any of you has a grievance against someone. Forgive as the Lord forgave you.* [14] *And over all these virtues put on love, which binds them all together in perfect unity.*
> *(Colossians 3 v 12-14)*

The five virtues of verse 12 are all other-person centred, but two things are highlighted in particular in verse 13: that we need to "bear with" and "forgive" one another. There is biblical honesty here. Our friends will let us down. If you are only looking for friends who will love you perfectly, then I'm afraid you'll never have any friends at all.

As one young woman at our church observed, "I think that some of us here are less willing to forgive our friends than we would be a spouse. When husbands are thoughtless, we can tend to roll our eyes, with a 'Well, what do you expect?' But when our friends let us down, our response can be 'I'm done with her. I'm cutting her out of my life.'"

Maybe this attitude comes from a very high view of friendship. Yet it's an unrealistic one. So be ready to forgive your friends.

5. Can I Give You a Hug?

Some of you are going to hate this, but....

For some people who feel they are lacking family and close relationships, one thing they miss is human touch. Different cultures have very different expectations of physical contact, but when we look at the Bible, we see that touch is clearly important. Jesus surprised people by touching, among others, a leper (Matthew 8 v 3), a woman with a fever (Matthew 8 v 15), a blind man (Matthew 9 v 29), the disciples when terrified (Matthew 17 v 7), the tongue of a mute man (Mark 7 v 33), the funeral bier of a dead man (Luke 7 v 14), and a known prostitute (Luke 7 v 39). He didn't *need* to touch anyone to heal them, but it was a sign of compassion and care. And that much is still true today.

This is mostly straightforward with members of the same sex. But when it comes to members of the opposite sex, in our Western church culture a good and right concern not to be inappropriate has sometimes led us to view every man or woman as a dangerous source of potential temptation. Yet the Bible calls us to view one another as brothers and sisters—and when we get this dynamic right, we can enjoy warm, but appropriate, familial relationships. As Paul tells a younger church leader, Timothy:

> *Treat younger men as brothers, older women as mothers, and younger women as sisters, with absolute purity.*
>
> *(1 Timothy 5 v 1-2)*

In an era of #metoo, this is culturally tricky. Sensitivity, care and wisdom are needed. But it would be a great pity if the church came to the conclusion that every single touch is a danger. And on the other hand, it would be great if we could avoid romanticising every touch or action too.

So while we must not be naïve, bodily contact matters. Hugs are important! We should try to find a culturally acceptable way of caring for others in this way. I know, I know, this makes some of us awkward. But go on. Give it a go. Not with everyone! But especially with good friends who are single, when they offer a hand or a wave of greeting, why not suggest, "C'mon, give me a hug!"?

Friendship is one of life's great treasures. For those who are denying their desires for relational intimacy which fall outside of biblical teaching, then friendship will be one of the ways that Jesus' promise of one-hundred-fold blessing will be realised. And for those who are cut off from their families (or just living a long way away), Christian friends are their only family, practically speaking.

So, for those of us who do find ourselves happily in families or friendship groups, here is a call to make those families and groups more porous. We should be outward looking like the Trinity. We can't even begin to imagine the intensity of love between the Father, Son and Spirit, and yet still they say, *Join us*. We ought to have families which echo that attitude and love.

For those who still struggle to believe Jesus' promise, I'm sorry if you feel you've been let down. It may be that you have. But please bear with others and forgive them.

Jesus does not make promises that are untrue. There can be no losers in church.

10. ONLINE: TRUE TO SELFIE IN A VIRTUAL WORLD

"Beauty is the battlefield where God and Satan contend with each other for the hearts of men"
Dostoevsky, *The Brothers Karamazov*

Sara Melotti was a fashion photographer in New York. She had a good client base and earned decent money. Yet she started to feel uneasy about her profession. Her day job was to produce images of unrealistic beauty, with the aid of lighting, makeup and photoshopping. Yet in the evenings, all of her friends complained about their appearance, and Sara herself had reached the point where she couldn't look in a mirror without wanting to photoshop her own face. This conflict between her job and her life started to rankle until the point where she quit, saying that she no longer wanted to be part of the machine causing women to have low self-esteem.

Sara took some time off to travel and, almost unthinkingly, began posting beautifully curated photos of herself in exotic locations. She rapidly developed a loyal and large number of followers on Instagram and made a living as an "influencer". Yet in her words, she again started to feel a little queasy. She began to question herself and fellow travel instagrammers: "What are we doing with our lives? None of us have stayed to drink in the beauty, to talk to the locals selling souvenirs, to enjoy the moment. We've taken our photo and left. It's all so vacuous it makes me feel sad. My travel photos on Instagram were setting unrealistic expectations. They didn't depict real life."[22]

Although I don't post much, I really do love social media. I so appreciate being able see what friends are up to in other parts of the country or on the other side of the world. But there is a great irony that in a culture which increasingly encourages everyone to be true to themselves, people are going to ever greater lengths to alter reality online.

One bestselling book of the past few years has the stark title: *Everybody Lies: What the Internet Can Tell Us about Who We Really Are.* It's by the data scientist Seth Stephens-Davidowitz. The book pulls together research to show, among other things, that there is a gulf between how people describe themselves on social media and the things they search for online. So, someone may describe themselves as an avid sports fan, yet all their internet searches are on taxidermy. Someone may describe themselves as happily married, but their search history is dominated by porn.

That may not come as much of a surprise. But we do need to stop and think about what impact that has.

Most 21st-century people would declare their love of truth, happiness and community, yet when we immerse ourselves in social media, we risk becoming lost in a world of distortion, jealousy and loneliness. Perhaps you feel that you already are. You feel a gnawing sense of uneasy dissatisfaction every time you scroll through Instagram or open up Snapchat. But you do it anyway.

So what would it take for us to be genuinely "true to self" online? I mean that in the straightforward sense of telling the truth, showing the truth, and valuing the truth. Because when "everybody lies", everybody loses. How then can we navigate our online and offline relationships in a way that cultivates the kind of friendships which, as we've already seen, we all really need—and which we're designed for as image-bearers? We're going to look at two contrasts in this chapter: [1] editing ourselves v. being honest and [2] safe loneliness v. risky blessing.

How Can We Be Real Anymore?

It was only back in 2010 that Apple introduced the front-facing camera onto their iPhone. The original intention was that it would facilitate FaceTime calls. Its main purpose rapidly became the selfie. Within four years, humanity was taking over a billion selfies every day! At the extreme end, people are so keen to take a photo of themselves doing something exciting that there are now more than 60 deaths per year involving people taking selfies. You are more likely to die taking a selfie than you are from being attacked by a shark! Things became so bad in Russia that they ran a state-sponsored, "Safe Selfie" campaign. It had the tagline "Even a million likes are not worth your life". Well, quite.

That's extreme. Most people's pursuit of the perfect selfie is far more subtle. Maybe you're among the 48-68% of adults who edit your selfies before sharing them with anyone else. (The figure varies depending on the surveys.) That means that at least half of the photos we see have been photoshopped in some way. Not just celebrities, not just fashion shoots, but regular Joes; our friends; our family.

Why all the touching up? I reckon that at least part of it comes down to the desire for "likes". I've had some people admit to me that they have become somewhat addicted to social-media approval. They post something and wait desperately for likes to follow. Their outlook on their whole day depends on the reaction from their friends. Some go to extraordinary lengths and buy followers on Buzzoid, who will automatically like and comment on things you post.

So, there are two separate but very much connected phenomena here: a world longing for "likes" and the editing of pictures to produce them. Both are pretty unhealthy.

If we take a step back for a moment, we can see that this is part of a wider tendency in the West to worship the body. It's almost impossible to open a magazine or newspaper without voluminous pages focusing on the body—what to put on or take off it. How to improve it, remodel it, sculpt it.

My weekend paper had a recent feature: "A bloke's guide to summer". It opened by saying, "Guys, remember when all you needed to do when the sun shone was break out a Hawaiian shirt and put some beers on ice? Now, so much more is required: ribbed abs, tight trunks, waxed torso—and expert barbecue skills".[23] Yet my guess is that even as the writing bemoaned that fact, all of the photos accompanying the article had been edited.

Something has indeed shifted: there is now far more attention paid to how we look. It's no wonder, then, that in a survey of 11-16-year-olds by the youth charity YMCA, 62% said they felt anxiety about how they would look in photos. Surely that's a sign that our culture's message on what bodies should be like has gone seriously awry.

Beauty – Truth = Ugliness

So what is the Bible's message on our appearance? For centuries, Christians have recognised that beauty must be allied with truth and goodness. The Bible doesn't actually use the word "beauty" very much. (It tends to be more concerned with "glory".) But in an essay on beauty, the seminary president Al Mohler makes the point that all of the Bible passages which describe the Lord as beautiful are describing his goodness. They focus not upon his physical attributes (how would you?) but upon his character. Take as one example Psalm 96:

> *For great is the LORD, and greatly to be praised;*
> *he is to be feared above all gods.*
> *For all the gods of the peoples are worthless idols,*
> *but the LORD made the heavens.*
> *Splendour and majesty are before him;*
> *strength and beauty are in his sanctuary.*
>
> *(Psalm 96 v 4-6, ESV)*

There is a moral context to beauty. You cannot call something beautiful which is not true or good. And you cannot call something good which is not true or beautiful. But when beauty meets with truth and goodness, then it really is wonderful. Perhaps it's simplest to write this as an equation:

Beauty – truth and goodness = ugliness

In this sense, an attractive woman in an airbrushed photograph cannot be described as *beautiful*, as this is not *true* beauty.

So here's a challenge for you—a way to really, *actually* apply what you're reading in this chapter: stop editing your pictures. Don't even add a filter.

And if that thought horrifies you, stop and ask yourself why that is. ("Because everyone else does"? "But it's winter and I'll look pasty"?)

Then stop and think about what that tells you.

Seriously—take time to engage with this little "thought experiment".

Now, the Bible does commend beauty, and there's no virtue in becoming as dowdy as possible. The Scriptures have nothing positive to say about the slovenly man or unkempt woman. Yet we mustn't miss its challenge on how much we care about physical appearance. At the risk of stating the obvious, the most attractive person in the Bible did not feel the need to alter his image:

> *He grew up before him like a tender shoot,*
> *and like a root out of dry ground.*
> *He had no beauty or majesty to attract us to him,*
> *nothing in his appearance that we should desire him.*
> *He was despised and rejected by mankind,*
> *a man of suffering, and familiar with pain.*
> *Like one from whom people hide their faces*
> *he was despised, and we held him in low esteem.*
> *(Isaiah 53 v 2-3)*

Jesus was a man who was true to himself and true to others. He was "real" with everyone: no pretence, no exaggeration, no airbrushing or touching up. In his speech he never sugarcoated the truth. In the last chapter we thought of his blunt warning that you have to give up a lot to follow him. Jesus would have been difficult to work for if you were a PR agency, always wanting to present your client in the most appealing light. And yet there is something undeniably attractive about this man of complete integrity. His followers are called to be people of integrity too.

Truth About Every Believer

It's one thing to tell you to stop posting fake photos, or to tell you to stop obsessing over your appearance. But telling someone to "stop it" rarely helps them to. Instead, we need a bigger truth to capture our hearts. We need to feel a better sense of approval than we get from likes on a post. We need a more permanent boost to our confidence than we can get from the ping of a notification. That's why I'm asking you to pause and consider a number of truths about who you are in Christ. Read them slowly to yourself.

I have life (John 1 v 4).

I have light (John 1 v 4).

I am bearing fruit (John 15 v 4).

I have joy (John 16 v 22).

I am dead to sin (Romans 6 v 11).

I am alive to God (Romans 6 v 11).

I have eternal life (Romans 6 v 23).

I am under no condemnation (Romans 8 v 1).

I cannot be separated from God's love (Romans 8 v 39).

I am sanctified (1 Corinthians 1 v 2).

I have received grace (1 Corinthians 1 v 4).

I belong to God's community (1 Corinthians 12 v 27).

I have the sure hope of resurrection (1 Corinthians 15 v 22).

I am a new creation (2 Corinthians 5 v 17).

I am reconciled to God (2 Corinthians 5 v 19).

I am free (Galatians 2 v 4).

I am justified (Galatians 2 v 16).

I am one with my brothers and sisters (Galatians 3 v 28).

I have every spiritual blessing (Ephesians 1 v 3).

I am chosen (Ephesians 1 v 4).

I am adopted (Ephesians 1 v 5).

I am predestined (Ephesians 1 v 5).

I am redeemed (Ephesians 1 v 7).

I am raised and seated with Christ in the heavenly realms (Ephesians 2 v 6).

I am created for good works (Ephesians 2 v 10).

I have fullness (Colossians 2 v 10).

I am dearly loved (Colossians 3 v 12).

I have righteousness from God (Philippians 3 v 9).

I have glorious riches (Philippians 4 v 19).

These are the truths that mean we are beautiful and valuable and noticed—and it's all God's gift.

You may know all of this. You may give thanks for it every day. But when it comes to our lives online, these are the truths which really are worth shouting out to the world. We have some people at my church who are fantastic social-media evangelists, sharing both videos and pictures they've created alongside their joy in Christ. You may not think anyone wants to see you post this truth online, but why not try—winsomely and joyfully, without being unnecessarily weird—to do that today?

Real Life Is Risky

So social media often pressures us to edit ourselves, whereas the gospel calls us to be honest. But let's not throw the baby out with the bathwater. After all, at its best, social media is all about connecting us. And that's good, right?

Well, yes. In theory. But the reality turns out to be more complex. For instance, Jean Twenge's research shows that teens who visit social networking sites are more likely to tick the statements "I often feel lonely", "I often feel left out of things" and "I often wish I had more friends".[24] As one journalist put it, "As kids they were given the keys to the digital kingdom, but teenagers now feel lost inside".[25]

And perhaps the way we communicate is part of the problem. I read a striking piece by 24-year-old journalist Eleanor Halls. She and her friends refer to themselves as "Generation Mute" because they rarely speak on the phone and feel far more comfortable having a conversation via WhatsApp or Snapchat. She writes: "Generation Mute would rather not have a chat and a cup of tea … because with real conversation comes conflict, risk and vulnerability. And while our virtual bubbles may be lonely, at least they're safe."[26] Is that temptation to withdraw to "safe" ways of communicating something you've felt?

Let's stay with that thought and ask, "What is the risk you're feeling?" A fear of rejection? Opening up and being greeted with indifference? The discovery that when we're vulnerable, someone may hurt us?

And truthfully, those things might happen. The risk is real. But risk in relationships is good! Vulnerability creates a far richer, deeper friendship.

The problem with avoiding the risk of being hurt is that you can never know the joy of being loved by great friends. J.K. Rowling's strange gothic tale *The Warlock's Hairy Heart* tells of a handsome, skilled warlock who thinks solitude is better than ever falling in love. So, he removes his heart with magic and locks it up in a casket. But when he changes his mind and wants to marry, he returns to the casket, only to find his heart shrivelled and covered in black hair. He is no longer capable of truly loving.

The moral of the tale is that to protect yourself you must become cold and indifferent to others. But to love is to be vulnerable and involved.

There have been guys I've known who took a risk early in our friendship and told me about their history of alcoholism or battles with depression. When someone does that, you can get to honesty really quickly. While you can't open up with everyone you meet, that kind of vulnerability with a few means you are far less likely to fear rejection going forward. You know they'll accept you. You know they'll be patient with you. You know they'll forgive you.

The joy in the Christian life is not *just* that in a church there are different types of people with different opinions, but that we can relate to one another as forgiven sinners. We know that each and every one of us is morally flawed, but we don't have to airbrush our character faults. That list of things, which is true for you, is also true for them. We're not to flaunt our failures, but we can confess our failures. We don't have to hide or edit. We can be real. We can be true.

Churches Are Messy

A couple of years ago Facebook founder Mark Zuckerberg caused a little titter when he made a speech suggesting that the social-media site could fill the gap in people's lives left by the decline of churches and other communities. He suggested that "a lot of people now need to find a sense of purpose and support somewhere else".[27]

But you can't get that online in the same way you can in a church, where you are happily forced into friendships with people different to you. Churches are wonderfully messy! They are not organised by an algorithm, so that you only meet like-minded people. They are not designed to present information specifically to your individual tastes. Church prevents us from simply hanging out with PLUs (people like us). That means our views are challenged, our opinions are changed, and our blind spots are revealed. More than that, the rough edges of our characters can be smoothed. Committing to a church stirs us out of being self-serving and shapes us into people who are self-giving. Unlike Facebook, church tells us that the world does not revolve around "me".

This has never been more important. One piece of recent research highlighted how delusional we can be about our range of friends and influences. Ipsos Mori interviewed 19,000 people across 27 countries. The headline outcome was that 65% believed that *other people* lived in an online bubble and only listened to opinions they liked, but only 34% thought that they themselves lived in a similar bubble. We think we listen to a wider range of voices than we do in reality. But we need a mix of voices to reveal where we're wrong! We need a variety of people to show us our sins, not just individually but as a society.

The film *Bohemian Rhapsody* follows the fortunes of Freddie Mercury, the former frontman of the British rock band Queen. There's a poignant scene when Mercury returns to the band after attempting a solo project and makes his confession to the other three members:

"I hired a bunch of guys. I told them exactly what I wanted them to do and the problem was... they did it. No pushback

from Roger. None of your rewrites, Brian. None of his funny looks. I need you. And you need me."

When you hide yourself away from criticism and from hurt, you can be safe, but you'll never grow as you're meant to. You'll never change like you're supposed to. You'll never achieve what you could do.

Let me mention here just a couple of benefits that Proverbs highlights about honest counsel from other believers.

1. Honest Advice

The soothing tongue is a tree of life,
but a perverse tongue crushes the spirit.   (15 v 4)

Wounds from a friend can be trusted,
but an enemy multiplies kisses.   (27 v 6)

Words from an honest and kind tongue are like a tree of life—they can take us back to the Garden of Eden. The contrast is with deceit. So, the writer implies that a community where there is honesty is one without shame or pretence—one where we don't have to cover ourselves up morally. Honesty can begin to reproduce paradise!

We need to have friends who love us enough to wound us, not just send us a thumbs-up. I still value the friendship of a guy who said to me as a 20-year-old, "Matt, do you mind if I say something to you?" (That's the sort of question that you know precedes some tough love.) He went on to say, "You have the most wonderful zeal for the truth as a

Christian. Never lose that; it's precious. Now, if you could only combine that zeal with love for people, you would stop being obnoxious and do great good."

Now that's a wound... but from a friend. He was completely concerned with my best interest. You can't have that conversation through emojis!

2. A Variety of Opinions

For lack of guidance a nation falls,
>*but victory is won through many advisors. (11 v 14)*

Plans fail for lack of counsel,
>*but with many advisors they succeed.   (15 v 22)*

Listen to advice and accept discipline,
>*and at the end you will be counted among the wise.*
>>*(19 v 20)*

Taking advice from others is a massive theme in Proverbs. There is an emphasis on listening to "many" before taking a significant decision. I keep banging this drum with younger guys or couples at church. They'll make a big decision, but when they are asked, "Who did you chat this through with?" the response is often "Err, no one really". Yet the wisdom in a church family is priceless. Make sure you take advantage of the counsel of people of different ages. Older normally does mean wiser.

I always encourage people to make sure they take advice from someone they expect to disagree with them too. If you're Little Miss Risk-taker, then make sure you speak to Mrs Safe. If you're Mr Safe, then it's worth asking Monsieur Risky. You get the idea!

Everybody Wins

So, may I encourage you...

The next time you hear that a friend is low, or they send you a message with glum emojis, don't text them back; give them a call. Suggest that you meet up. It's what they really need, and it will build a far deeper friendship.

When you're tempted to cover up some immoral behaviour and live as a hypocrite, go to a friend who you know will wound you with the gospel. They will tell you to repent, but they will assure you that you can be forgiven.

When you're tempted to hang out only with people like you at church, make a conscious effort to befriend someone very different. Let their views challenge yours. Discover the blessing of having very little in common except Christ, and therefore still sharing the most precious truth and person in the world.

The online world of selfies and idyllic travel snaps is not a real world where we can find the honest relationships we want. Rich community is not found online but in a healthy church. You have to invest in face-to-face relationships. True happiness doesn't come from your picture being liked but from your soul being loved—

primarily by Jesus and then by friends who know you. When "everybody lies", then everybody loses. But when a Christian church can be honest with one another and allow wounds to come from people they know and trust deeply, then everybody wins.

11. I'M NOT THE MESSIAH...
[BUT I WANT TO BECOME
LIKE HIM]

*"Dream no small dreams for they stir
not the hearts of men."*
Von Goethe

Years ago, I remember reading a little blog piece that made me laugh out loud. It was called "An un-messianic sense of non-destiny" and was written by the scholar Carl Trueman. The gist of it was that having hit 40 years old, he had experienced a mild mid-life crisis (complete with a new sports car). In essence, Carl realised that he was not going to change the world. He was unremarkable:

"I woke up ... and realized that, if I was hit by a bus that night, whatever academic contribution I was ever going to make had already been made; I had done it; I need not worry about it anymore. I could, of course, continue grinding the stuff out, like some intellectual sausage machine; but it would be more of the same, variations on

a theme I had already played. No, an early Trueman death would not deprive the world of some great insight it might otherwise miss."[28]

He wrote that this realisation, although initially disappointing, was actually quite liberating: he was not particularly special and, in many ways, could very easily be replaced. He encouraged his readers that we would all be far happier with a similar "un-messianic sense of non-destiny".

After all, at the risk of sounding obvious, there's only one Messiah: Jesus. And he is magnificent. The history of the world is supremely the history of his kingdom. Although he is denied by many, he is the King of kings, and one day everyone will recognise that truth and worship him in his glory.

Compared to him, we are... well, unremarkable.

But the fact that he cares about us—now *that* is remarkable.

The truth that we can belong to his kingdom—that's *even more* remarkable.

The promise that in some sense we will rule with him in his kingdom one day—that's wonderfully and eternally remarkable!

But me, personally? I am not remarkable.

As individuals, we are inherently small and insignificant. But when we belong to Jesus, we're part of the most significant thing that is happening in the universe. In fact, it is really the only thing that is happening. With apologies to Hugh Jackman and the rest of the cast of *The Greatest Showman*, belonging to Jesus: *this* is the greatest show.

In short, we need to recognise that the world does not revolve around us. It revolves around Jesus. Yet in him we will find a contentment and purpose far grander than we ever could on our own.

Throughout this book, we've seen that our true identity is given to us, not created by us. In this last chapter we'll pull together some final conclusions on what that means for how we live our lives.

1. Live for a Bigger Story

Modern thrillers seem to have become smaller somehow. Whereas once upon a time James Bond would have saved the world from global catastrophe, now he has family and personal problems. In *Skyfall* he tries to save his "mum" (Judy Dench as M) from Javier Bardem's character, who was a sort of spy-brother to him. Then in *Spectre* he discovers that Ernst Blofeld and SPECTRE were only *partly* concerned with world domination—behind that, this classic baddie was driven by a hatred of Bond, because Blofeld's daddy had loved Bond more than him. While family conflict can make good film drama, there's a certain irony in the fact that the Bond saga has started to follow its parody, the *Austin Powers* series, in shrinking the narrative down to personal and family feuds.

Don't mishear me: I still loved the recent Bond films, but there's something very modern about fighting for yourself and your family, rather than the more "traditional" heroism of yesteryear's Bond, who would risk his life simply for queen and country—a cause which didn't affect him personally but was good for the world. (Oh well, at least there's still Ethan Hunt and the *Mission Impossible* franchise. He still saves the world!)

If many modern action films have smaller narratives, then maybe that is also true for some of us in our lives. We've lost the grand dream, the big ambition, the longing to give our lives to something that matters.

In 1940 – 1941, Britain endured an intense bombing campaign at the hands of the Germans, which came to be known as "the Blitz". 70+ years on, Brits still celebrate the idea of the "Blitz spirit" in the national collective memory. The notion of Londoners standing shoulder to shoulder in defiance of nightly bombing raids has become a deeply cherished part of British folklore.

Given that it was a time when Londoners faced danger and destruction every night, this rosy view of the Blitz is a little bizarre. Yet a generation of Brits remember it as a time when the industrial strikes, class struggles and the north-south division of the previous decade were put aside, and people came together in a common cause. They were united in making sacrifices for something nobler and greater than their own lives—and it brought happiness!

Christians really shouldn't be surprised. It's how we were designed to operate. And serving Jesus Christ is certainly a far grander mission than spending lots of time on "project me", or even winning a war. It affects the world and it lasts for ever! Just consider the beginning and end of the book of Revelation:

Jesus Christ ... is the faithful witness, the firstborn from the dead, and the ruler of the kings of the earth. To him who loves us and has freed us from our sins by his blood, and has made us to be a kingdom and priests to serve his God and Father—to him be glory and power for ever and ever! Amen.   *(Revelation 1 v 5-6)*

I did not see a temple in the city, because the Lord God Almighty and the Lamb are its temple. The city does not need the sun or the moon to shine on it, for the glory of God gives it light, and the Lamb is its lamp.

(Revelation 21 v 22-23)

Revelation was written by the apostle John to first-century Christians, who were tempted to compromise or give up on the faith. The massive encouragement is that if you serve Jesus, you are on the winning team—and so it's worth giving up anything for him. Chapter 1 opens with a vision of who Jesus is—to help us see Jesus and ourselves in our rightful places.

First, we're told that Jesus is the "faithful witness" (1 v 5). We live in a culture where people want to tell their stories; they want to share how they've been hurt or marginalised.

When we hear these stories, we're rightly moved by them. Yet very often there's an opposite story that is just as emotional and moving. So what do we do? It's no good trying to play a game of competitive hurt: "I feel more wronged than you" or "I suffer more discrimination than you". We need the faithful witness, who tells us the truth about ourselves and about the world. We need to listen to him.

Second, Jesus is the "firstborn from the dead"—proving that resurrection is possible and guaranteeing that we will rise too if we trust in him. We need to know that in a world which is so focused on the here and now, and which urges us to make sure we don't miss out. But we Christians can deny ourselves in the knowledge that this world is fleeting, this current age is passing away, and that we have been designed to find perfect contentment in the next.

Third, Jesus is the "ruler of the kings of the earth". There is no one who can successfully contest his rule, any more than a solitary ant could beat an Olympic sprinter in a race.

That means it's all about him. *He* is the one who loves us though we are undeserving. *He* has set his followers free from sin and condemnation though his bloody atoning death. *He* has made us into his kingdom and into priests who serve him and speak of him.

We were nothing. *He* has made us everything. And so it is right that glory and power go to him for ever and ever (and not to us).

Yet deep down, we find this hard to accept. Back in 1958 C.S. Lewis observed:

"There remains [in us] some lingering idea of our own, our very own attractiveness. It is easy to acknowledge, but almost impossible to realise for long, that we are mirrors whose brightness, if we are bright, is wholly derived from the sun that shines upon us. Surely, we must have a little— however little—native luminosity? Surely, we can't be quite creatures?" (C.S. Lewis, The Four Loves, p 131)

Something warped within humanity has *always* wanted to say, "Look at me, look at me!" And now in the West we live in a time of expressive individualism, when it's deemed a virtue to say, "Look at me". No wonder it's a popular philosophy!

But, we're only mirrors. We shine brightest when we look at him. In the picture of the new creation in Revelation 21, there is no sun or moon because Jesus is the source of all light. It's when we look at him that we shine, that we find our greatest joy, that we are truly true to self. Serving him means giving our lives to a kingdom that will last for ever. It means we're part of a bigger cause, a better story, a higher calling. And deep down, that's what we want most.

2. Enjoy the Freedom of Boundaries

Most of us assume that freedom is good. Freedom of speech? (Tick.) Freedom to explore? (Tick.) Freedom of self-expression? (Tick.) In the West, our brains work on this default setting: freedom = good; restriction = bad.

At the same time, we recognise that boundaries can also be good in some settings. Motor-racing drivers don't complain about safety barriers around the track: "I feel constrained by the barriers. They restrict my freedom to explore." They'd be more likely to think: "Phew, the barriers mean I can enjoy driving at 200mph. They keep me on the track where I can experience the phenomenal exhilaration of high speeds and take controlled risks to overtake other drivers. They stop me driving off into spectators or surfaces where I'll get a puncture."

In the same way, God gives us rules so that we are free to live life to the full. Life spent following Jesus is exhilarating, and we can take risks, but if we live within the parameters he gives us, then we're safe. We won't do significant damage to ourselves or others.

By contrast, when we live ignoring God's boundaries, we risk harming ourselves or others. Without any parameters on how we should live, we are cast adrift on an endless ocean of emotional angst, uncertain of where we're heading or what we will find. For a while this "freedom" may seem exciting, but everyone eventually reaches a point where they want to find dry land. They want to land upon solid convictions about who they are and how they should live.

As one example, I was struck by this comment made by Clare Foges, writing in *The Times* about adults giving children the "freedom" to choose their gender:

"Children thrive on stability and are made anxious by chaos and blurred boundaries. Instead of 'liberating' children from social constructs, the new orthodoxy on gender identity gives them the burden of endless choice and introspection to work out what they really are ... While some would argue that the 'old-fashioned' way of classifying children as boys or girls (according to biology) is restrictive, I would counter that for the vast majority of children it is liberating. It frees you from endless negotiation with yourself about what you are."[29]

That's a freedom that we used to take for granted: freedom from "endless negotiation with yourself about what you are". But I'm not suggesting we return to an "old-fashioned" system of identities. Rather, as we've seen, we need to listen to the Creator, as he tells us who we are.

The Bible is unashamed in asserting that following God's word brings freedom:

Anyone who listens to the word but does not do what it says is like someone who looks at his face in a mirror and, after looking at himself, goes away and immediately forgets what he looks like. But whoever looks intently into the perfect law that gives freedom and continues in it—not forgetting what they have heard but doing it—they will be blessed in what they do.   *(James 1 v 23-25)*

"The perfect law that gives freedom." I wonder if you view God's word in that way? I taught the Ten Commandments recently as a series at church. I'd never done that before, but what struck me was actually how liberating they are. They're broad principles to shape God's people and keep us free. They're not detailed prescriptions to kill our joy.

You might think of them as lines on a sports pitch. If you tried to have a game of tennis without any lines, it would be rubbish. You would end up arguing with your opponent about whether each shot was in or out. You couldn't take pleasure in hitting a beautiful shot that only just dropped in. You would probably end up in a competition simply to see who could hit the ball hardest.

But, add a few white lines—add a few laws—and you can have enormous pleasure in playing.

When I was preparing to preach through the Ten Commandments, one thing that became clear was that they were taught a lot more regularly in previous generations. In particular, the Puritan writers of the 17th century considered the Ten Commandments and their implications to be a key part of the Christian basics. What did they write a lot less about? Guidance. It seems that Christians then didn't have lots of questions about guidance: "What should I do? How should I live?" But these days, when the teaching of the law has been neglected, lots of Christians are paralysed by the uncertainty of what to do next. Perhaps the Puritans teach us that when we accept God's broad parameters for life, we are liberated to get on with living!

God's word gives freedom. When we reject him and his boundaries, we end up uncertain of where we're meant to be heading and we struggle for cohesion in our communities. But when we embrace the boundaries that our good and loving Creator has given us, it gives perfect freedom.

3. Become Ever More Glorious

In chapter 2 we looked at Psalm 8 and saw three connected truths that make sense of our human condition: we're not gods, but we do wear crowns... but they're crowns which are cracked by sin. Mercifully, God is in the business of restoring us. And, as C.S. Lewis observed, the way to shine more brightly—the way to become more glorious—is not to try to turn up our own wattage but to reflect the glory of Christ. As Paul writes:

And we all, who with unveiled faces contemplate [or reflect] the Lord's glory, are being transformed into his image with ever-increasing glory, which comes from the Lord, who is the Spirit.   *(2 Corinthians 3 v 18)*

Paul is encouraging his readers to have confidence in his gospel message. At that time, some church leaders in Corinth were peddling a message of self-promotion. But Paul explains that it is only in looking to Christ and trusting in *him* that our hearts are transformed in new birth.

And as we go on in the Christian life, it is as we continue to contemplate or reflect Jesus' glory that we gradually become more like him. That's how our cracked crowns will be repaired. It is as we look to Christ—the one who is crowned with supreme glory (Psalm 8)—that we become more like the people God made us to be, reflecting his image to the world.

If you set your body in the summer sun, you'll be transformed by melanin in the skin and end up darker-skinned. If you fix your ears on a certain tune, it will enter your subconscious, and you'll end up singing it in the shower. If you focus your time with a group of people with very strong accents, you'll end up speaking like them. And as you fix your eyes on Jesus and behold the glory of God in Christ, you'll be transformed and end up with a character like his. You don't have to settle for the way you are or despair at the fact that change never comes. You really will grow more joyful, more patient, more compassionate, more kind. God is changing us, here and now, as we gaze at Jesus.

The last time I heard the late preacher John Stott speak was at a convention in London, when his subject was the uniqueness of Christ. I think he adapted the quote of another, but he put it brilliantly:

"We may speak, if we will, of Alexander the Great, and Charles the Great, and Napoleon the Great, but not Jesus the Great. He is not the Great. He is Jesus the Only. There is nobody like him. He has no peers. He has no rivals. And he has no successors. So our place is on our faces, prostrate before him in humble adoration and praise."

It's when we're on our knees before him, reflecting him, that we are truly human.

This process of being restored to God's image will never be complete in this life. We await its fulfilment in the new creation—the home of glory. Until then, we can rightly observe with John Newton:

"I am not what I ought to be ... I am not what I wish to be ... I am not what I hope to be [in another world]. Yet ... I am not what I once was ... [and] 'by the grace of God I am what I am.'"

True to Self?

Our culture tells us that happiness is found when we look within to find who we are. We're told that we need to boost our self-esteem. We're encouraged to find god within ourselves and told that we can worship ourselves.

These are such deep-rooted assumptions that few want to listen to the emerging data which says it's not true. This philosophy is not producing happiness, because none of us are *that* exciting.

The Bible has always insisted that we're made for so much more. Being true to ourselves must involve being true to our original design and working with the grain of how the good Creator God has made us, rather than bending ourselves out of shape.

Being true to self should also mean that we can be honest about our desires for relationships and our longings for purpose—yet also honest about our failings and poor motives. The joy of forgiveness in Christianity is that we can be completely honest about who we are, yet also know we are truly loved and valued by God our Father.

In our culture people are always striving for perfection. We've discussed the pursuit of the perfect selfie: the photoshopped flawlessness that we're told to aspire to. Yet Jesus holds out the *attainable* hope of perfection. In this life we can begin to be transformed, but one day we will be like him.

As one author put it, in Jesus there is true character:

"He is tenderness without weakness, strength without harshness, humility without the slightest lack of confidence, holiness and unbending convictions without the slightest lack of approachability, power without insensitivity, passion without prejudice. There is never a false step, never a jarring note. This is life at the highest."[30]

One day we'll be restored to the full image of God, yet without losing our individuality. Rather, we'll be part of a rich tapestry as God gathers together people of every tribe and people and language; of every age and talent and gift; of every era of history and every corner of the earth. And in our extraordinary variety, we shall be like Jesus.

In this life we're moving closer to that each and every day as we deny ourselves and follow him. In that way we can be...

True to our longings

True to our ambitions

True in our relationships

True with ourselves

True to our design

Truly finding happiness

Truly enjoying freedom

Truly communicating

True to our purpose

True to our emotions

True to yourself.

ENDNOTES

1 Michelle Obama, "Remarks by the First Lady and Oprah Winfrey in a Conversation at the United State of Women Summit, 14 June 2016, https://obamawhitehouse.archives. gov/the-press-office/2016/06/14/remarks-first-lady-and-oprah-winfrey-conversation-united-state-women

2 Oprah Winfrey, "What Oprah Knows For Sure About Authenticity"; *O, The Oprah Magazine*, November 2015, http://www.oprah.com/inspiration/what-oprah-knows-for-sure-about-authenticity

3 Mike Brown, "Is Tinder a Match for Millennials?", 22 March 2017, https://lendedu.com/blog/tinder-match-millennials

4 BBC News, 03 December 2018, https://www.bbc.co.uk/news/world-europe-46425774

5 ITV News, 03 August 2016, https://www.itv.com/news/2016-08-03/transgender-woman-who-had-doubts-over-sex-change-found-dead/

6 Psychology Today, "Gender Dysphoria", https://www.psychologytoday.com/gb/conditions/gender-dysphoria

7 Galop, "Transphobia", http://www.galop.org.uk/transphobia

8 As quoted in "Times columnist complains to BBC about promoting transgender ideology", 28 September 2016, https://www.christianconcern.com/our-concerns/social/times-columnist-complains-to-bbc-about-promoting-transgender-ideology

9 American College of Pediatricians, "Normalizing Gender Dysphoria is Dangerous and Unethical", 03 August 2016, https://www.acpeds.org/normalizing-gender-dysphoria-is-dangerous-and-unethical

10 Pam Belluck, "Many Genes Influence Same-Sex Sexuality, Not a Single 'Gay Gene'", 29 August 2019, https://www.nytimes.com/2019/08/29/science/gay-gene-sex.html

11 International Women's Health Coalition, "Sexual Rights are Human Rights", https://iwhc.org/articles/sexual-rights-human-rights

12 Sirin Kale, "Erectile dysfunction or performance anxiety? The truth behind a modern malaise", 18 October 2018, https://www.theguardian.com/lifeandstyle/2018/oct/18/erectile-dysfunction-performance-anxiety-truth-modern-malaise

13 Allison Pearson, "Pornography has changed the landscape of adolescence beyond all recognition", 22 April 2015, https://www.telegraph.co.uk/women/mother-tongue/11554595/pornography-has-changed-the-landscape-of-adolescence-beyond-all-recognition.html

14 Harvey Cox, "Playboy's Doctrine of Male", https://www.religion-online.org/article/playboys-doctrine-of-male

15 As quoted in Steve Connor, "The Recipe for a Great Marriage has Changed", 13 February 2014, https://www.independent.co.uk/news/science/the-recipe-for-a-great-marriage-has-changed-partners-must-help-each-other-discover-inner-potential-9126130.html

16 Ada Calhoun, "The marriage dilemma: Is infidelity inevitable?", 11 June 2017, https://www.thetimes.co.uk/article/the-marriage-dilemma-is-infidelity-inevitable-bhkfqmtz7

17 Alain de Botton, "A Point of View: What's in a Marriage?", 22 July 2011, https://www.bbc.co.uk/news/

magazine-14248803

18 Nichi Hodgson, "If you're in a bad marriage, don't try to mend it—end it", 19 July 2018, https://www.theguardian. com/commentisfree/2018/jul/19/bad-marriage-unhappy-marriages-health

19 Juliet Samuel, "Shouldn't family be part of the 'British dream'?", 07 October 2017, https://www.telegraph.co.uk/ news/2017/10/07/shouldnt-family-part-british-dream

20 Rod Liddle, "Divorce is a disaster. Don't let's make it easier", 25 November 2017, https://www.spectator. co.uk/2017/11/divorce-destroys-society-dont-lets-make-it-easier/

21 Matt Moore, "The Perilous Sin of Affirming Sin," https:// mychristiandaily.com/perilous-sin-affirming-sin/ (accessed 17 July 2019)

22 Candice Habershone, "How it feels to... be a star on Instagram", 09 July 2017, https://www.thetimes.co.uk/ article/how-it-feels-to-be-a-star-on-instagram-kxgqqm9f6

23 "Tanned! Toned! Topless! A bloke's guide to summer", 15 July 2017, https://www.thetimes.co.uk/article/tanned-toned-topless-a-blokes-guide-to-summer-ldd3khmbf

24 Jean Twenge, "What's up with the iGeneration?", 02 September 2017, https://www.thetimes.co.uk/article/ whats-up-with-the-igeneration-q2hct3vxk

25 Helen Rumbelow, "We know what you're thinking: vain, anxious and selfie-obsessed", 06 November 2017, https:// www.thetimes.co.uk/article/we-know-what-youre-thinking-vain-anxious-and-selfieobsessed-tjrkfckq8

26 Eleanor Halls, "Welcome to generation mute", 05 November

2017, https://www.thetimes.co.uk/article/welcome-to-generation-mute-the-age-group-that-prefers-messaging-to-actual-conversation-m6kdgvnps

27 As quoted in Peter Ormerod, "Mark Zuckerberg, the Church of Facebook can never be. Here's why", 29 June 2017, https://www.theguardian.com/commentisfree/2017/jun/29/mark-zuckerberg-church-facebook-social-network

28 Carl Trueman, "An Unmessianic Sense of Non-Destiny", April 2010, http://www.reformation21.org/articles/an-unmessianic-sense-of-nondestiny.php

29 Clare Foges, "Gender-fluid world is muddling young minds", 27 July 2017, https://www.thetimes.co.uk/article/gender-fluid-world-is-muddling-young-minds-3cjdfk97l

30 John Watson, quoted in Timothy Keller, *Encounters with Jesus* (Hodder & Stoughton, 2014), chapter 3.

OTHER BOOKS CITED

Charles Darwin, *The Descent of Man* (John Murray, 1871)

Elizabeth Gilbert, *Eat, Pray, Love: One Woman's Search for Everything* (Bloomsbury, 2007)

Robert Greene, *The 48 Laws of Power* (Profile Books, 2000)

Stanley Grenz, *Sexual Ethics: An Evangelical Perspective* (Westminster John Knox Press, 1999)

CS Lewis, *The Four Loves* (Geoffrey Bles, 1960)

Ayn Rand, *Anthem* (Cassell, 1938, now available online for free via Project Gutenberg)

Will Storr, *Selfie: How the West Became Self-Obsessed* (Picador, 2018)

Matthew Syed, *The Greatest: What Sport Teaches Us About Achieving Success* (John Murray, 2017)

BIBLICAL | RELEVANT | ACCESSIBLE

At The Good Book Company, we are dedicated to helping Christians and local churches grow. We believe that God's growth process always starts with hearing clearly what he has said to us through his timeless word—the Bible.

Ever since we opened our doors in 1991, we have been striving to produce Bible-based resources that bring glory to God. We have grown to become an international provider of user-friendly resources to the Christian community, with believers of all backgrounds and denominations using our books, Bible studies, devotionals, evangelistic resources, and DVD-based courses.

We want to equip ordinary Christians to live for Christ day by day, and churches to grow in their knowledge of God, their love for one another, and the effectiveness of their outreach.

Call us for a discussion of your needs or visit one of our local websites for more information on the resources and services we provide.

Your friends at The Good Book Company

thegoodbook.com | thegoodbook.co.uk
thegoodbook.com.au | thegoodbook.co.nz
thegoodbook.co.in